Physical Characteristics of the Coton de Tuléar
(from the Fédération Cynologique Internationale breed standard)

Body: Topline very slightly convex. Dog longer than high. Withers: Only slightly pronounced. Back and loin: Strong back, topline very slightly arched. Loin well muscled. Croup: Oblique, short and muscled. Chest: Well developed, well let down to elbow level, long. Ribs well sprung. Belly: Tucked up but not excessively.

Tail: Low set, in the axis of the spinal column.

Hindquarters: The hindlegs are upright. Upper thigh: Strongly muscled. Lower thigh: Oblique, forming with the femur an angle of about 120°. Hock joint: Dry, well defined. Rear pastern: Vertical. Hindfeet: Similar to forefeet.

Size: Males: 26 to 28 cm, tolerance of 2 cm above and 1 cm below. Bitches: 23 to 25 cm, tolerance of 2 cm above and 1 cm below.

Weight: Males: From 4 kg to a maximum of 6 kg. Bitches: From 3.5 kg to a maximum of 5 kg.

Color: Ground color: White. A few slight shadings of light gray color (mixture of white and black hairs) or of red-roan (mixture of white and fawn hairs) are permitted on the ears.

Coton de Tuléar

By Wolfgang Knorr

Translated by Elké and Thomas Ulber

Contents

9   History of the Coton de Tuléar

Meet the canine royalty of Madagascar, the Coton de Tuléar. See how this rare member of the Bichon family developed on the island and made its way to other parts of the world, finding a niche for itself in France and a special place in the hearts of those lucky enough to know it.

17   Characteristics of the Coton de Tuléar

A charming clown in a cottony coat, the Coton is a dog with a huge personality that belies his small stature. Learn about the breed's delightful character and discuss basic requirements of owning a Coton to decide if this is the best dog for you...and vice-versa!

26   Breed Standard for the Coton de Tuléar

Learn the requirements of a well-bred Coton de Tuléar by studying the description of the breed set forth in the Fédération Cynologique Internationale's standard. Both show dogs and pets must possess key characteristics as outlined in the breed standard.

39   Your Puppy Coton de Tuléar

Be advised about choosing a reputable breeder and selecting a healthy, typical puppy. Understand the responsibilities of ownership, including home preparation, acclimatization, the vet and prevention of common puppy problems.

67   Everyday Care of Your Coton de Tuléar

Enter into a sensible discussion of dietary and feeding considerations, exercise, grooming, traveling and identification of your dog. This chapter discusses Coton de Tuléar care for all stages of development.

Training Your Coton de Tuléar   86

By Charlotte Schwartz
Be informed about the importance of training your Coton de Tuléar from the basics of housebreaking and understanding the development of a young dog to executing obedience commands (sit, stay, down, etc.).

Health Care of Your Coton de Tuléar   115

Discover how to select a qualified vet and care for your dog at all stages of life. Topics include vaccinations, skin problems, dealing with external and internal parasites and common medical and behavioral conditions.

Behavior of Your Coton de Tuléar   146

Learn to recognize and handle behavioral problems that may arise with your Coton de Tuléar. Topics discussed include separation anxiety, aggression, barking, chewing, digging, begging, jumping up and more.

Index 156

KENNEL CLUB BOOKS: COTON DE TULÉAR
ISBN: 1-59378-354-X

Copyright © 2005 • Kennel Club Books, LLC
308 Main Street, Allenhurst, NJ 07711 USA
Cover Design Patented: US 6,435,559 B2 • Printed in South Korea

Photos by Isabelle Français with additional photographs by:
Norvia Behling, T.J. Calhoun, Carolina Biological Supply, Viktoria Deak, Doskocil, James Hayden-Yoav, James R Hayden, RBP, Carol Ann Johnson, Bill Jonas, Dwight R. Kuhn, Dr. Dennis Kunkel, Mikki Pet Products, Phototake, Jean Claude Revy, Dr. Andrew Spielman and Alice van Kempen.

10 9 8 7 6 5 4 3 2

Deriving from Madagascar, the Coton de Tuléar possesses a cotton-like coat that distinguishes it from most other breeds of dog.

HISTORY OF THE

COTON DE TULÉAR

It is an onerous undertaking to try and describe a dog breed with competence when hardly any literature about the breed can be found, when the documentation that can be found is so sparsely distributed and when the breed's origin is, like that of many other dog breeds, everything but clear. Nevertheless, it is a worthwhile effort to investigate the subject as closely as possible and to introduce a most delightful dog breed, the Coton de Tuléar, to the readers of this book. Let us therefore try to shed some light on the origins of this breed, a breed that is not even mentioned in most books on dogs.

Many may say, "Coton de Tuléar, what a funny name for a dog!" In this case, the name is entirely appropriate. Found principally in the port city of Tuléar, this is a small Madagascan dog whose beautiful white or nearly all-white coat has—just like the ripe fruit of the cotton bush—a texture similar to a wad of cotton wool. The French word *coton* translates to the English *cotton*. The texture of the breed's coat makes the Coton stand out from almost all other dog breeds.

SAVE THE COTON!
With the Coton de Tuléar's being threatened by extinction, the Madagascan government imposed an export stop in 1992.

Madagascar, which later became the native country of the Coton, used to be a popular center of trade for many seafarers and merchants. These travelers often carried small dogs of the Bichon type on board their ships, where the dogs earned their keep as undemanding terminators of mice and rats. In the process, these dogs reached ports around the globe.

Our Coton de Tuléar is presumed to have evolved from these small Bichon-like native dogs, but what explanation is there for the variety of colors that can be found in the breed? Today's Cotons have the blood of the same ancestors as today's other Bichons, which clearly explains their white coat and their body shape. The original Bichons mingled with some stray terriers on the island, which placed a

Italy's Bichon breed, the Bolognese, is similar to the Coton and seen in a coat of pure white.

It is quite obvious that the Coton de Tuléar is closely related to the Bichon breeds. Its ancestors were probably introduced to the country by Indian troopers who found a new home on the Mauritian island of Bourbon around 1665. The neighboring island of La Réunion was home to the Chien Coton, also known as the Havana Silk Dog, and the Madagascan Cotton Dog or Cotton Swab Dog. Both bore a distinct resemblance to the Maltese, the Tenerife dog (today's Bichon Frise) and the Bolognese.

With its numerous ports,

MADAGASCAR, A LOST PARADISE

Madagascar is referred to as a bridge between two worlds, those worlds being Asia and Africa. It is an idyllic island, covering 581,540 sq km (about 224,500 square miles) of land surface with about 4,828 km (about 3,000 miles) of coastline and a range of climatic zones. It is marked by a many-tiered society. At present, the island is inhabited by some 15 million people, which averages to only about 25 people per square kilometer.

A southwestern trade wind, blowing in from the Indian Ocean, favors tropical rainforests, which are, however, under severe threat from human activity. Large areas are therefore now covered merely with scrub. The weather is dominated by the monsoon during the summer months, which makes way to winterly trade winds in the western lowlands. All central regions are marked by a pleasantly warm climate, while the south of the island presents itself rather arid.

The island is home to unbelievably diverse flora and fauna, the latter including a wealth of colorful butterflies, crocodiles, lemurs (small monkey-like primates) and the largest and smallest chameleons on earth. A visit to this eldorado creates the impression of walking straight through a book on evolutionary history. The towns may be peppered with scattered cornfields, manioc shrubs and banana plants, with shade being offered under the wide umbrella crowns of huge mango trees. The rich green of the lush vegetation is only enhanced by the purple-red flowers of the famous flamboyant trees.

The fact that temperature never drops below 68°F (20°C) here offers a plausible explanation for the light and airy coat of the Coton de Tuléar, despite its being most certainly not an original inhabitant of this dream island, but rather evolving from Bichon-like predecessors.

Viktoria Deak's Yatiare of Woodland Cottage is an 18-month-old bitch.

RECOGNITION IN EUROPE

The Coton de Tuléar was recognized by the Fédération Cynologique Internationale (FCI) as a distinct breed of Madagascan origin. It is a relatively new breed in terms of FCI recognition, this occurring in 1970. In Europe, the first Cotons appeared around 1975, when breeding with Cotons imported directly from Madagascar commenced in France. The breed was extremely rare and practically unknown to the public. The first three pups were entered into the French breeding register in 1976. By 1984, their number had increased to 192 pups, while at the same time only 15 specimens were known to exist on Madagascar; these had all been appraised by a recognized judge.

Hailing from France via Tenerife, the Bichon Frise is among the most famous of the Bichon breeds.

the Coton's arched back, longer legs and the two skin colors: gray and pink.

Madagascar was also home to a large number of Papillons bred in Belgium. These dogs were tri-colored in ginger, black and brown and may be responsible for some ears found in the Coton that tend to stand erect or are upright in the fashion of the Collie with the tips turned down.

After France claimed Madagascar in the 17th century, the island paradise also became home to the French aristocracy. Influenced by the literary ways of life that marked this epoch, aristocratic ladies found it fashionable to surround themselves with uncommon treasures. Therefore, it soon became unlawful by royal decree for a commoner to keep a Coton, making it a privilege reserved for those of noble birth and those related to the court on the island. It appears possible, though, that the first "cotton dogs" were actually given as presents to the regents of the island

little terrier "time bomb" in the white fluff and accounts for the Coton's inability to resist going after the neighbor's poor chickens! More precisely, it was Bedlington Terriers brought along by the French colonists that contributed

realm. The small Madagascan jewel thus was soon known as the "dog of royalty," and even today the Coton on Madagascar is kept mainly by residents of distinction.

This presumed history of the Coton is no doubt rather unspectacular, but at least quite realistic. Old legends, in contrast, may appear much more impressive, but can hardly be substantiated. One story tells of a pair of dogs that, kept afloat by their luxurious coats, reached the island of Madagascar by swimming after a ship carrying refugees was wrecked off the coast. How they made it through the multitude of sharks living in the waters around Madagascar remains unclear, however.

Other storytellers claim to be certain that European settlers brought along their spaniels, Maltese and Bolognese, which subsequently mingled with the dogs native to the island. What is sure, in any case, is that small white dogs have been living on this island for centuries. The name by which they subse-

SURVIVING THE ISLAND

It is presumed that many Cotons lived freely in their native country. They had to fend for themselves if they were to survive. Over time, they had acquired the skills to find food and managed to adapt to the climatic conditions. The dogs also had to learn to face dangers and outfox their main natural enemy on Madagascar, the crocodile. This skill was of particular importance if a Coton had to cross a river. The dog would bark loudly at one place at the bank to attract all of the crocodiles in the vicinity. Once the crocs arrived at that point, the dog would run some 100 meters (about 330 feet) down along the bank and swim across the river without being harmed.

Today, there are no more free-ranging Cotons on Madagascar, but locals who keep them are quick to report that the small dogs used to run free on the island in earlier times. The little vagabonds would beg for and receive kitchen scraps at houses so that their livelihood was ensured. Many hospitable families would not be able to resist these cute cuddly wads of cotton and would also give them shelter.

The Havanese, or Bichon Havanaise, derives from the tropical island country of Cuba and is gaining new admirers in America and Europe every day.

COTONS IN NORTH AMERICA

The Coton arrived in America in 1974, when Dr. Robert Jay Russell sent breeding stock over from Madagascar. The breed is rare in North America, and is not recognized by the American Kennel Club. There are devotees of the breed, though, with several clubs operating in the US and Canada. The first club in the US, the Coton de Tuléar Club of America (CTCA), founded by Dr. Russell, maintains its own breed standard. Other clubs abide by the FCI standard, including the United States of America Coton de Tuléar Club (USACTC), which is affiliated with the American Rare Breeds Association and the States Kennel Club.

quently became known was based on their hair, soft and aromatic like cotton, and the principal region in which they were found, the port city of Tuléar and the surrounding areas.

By careful selective breeding, Madagascan breeders have managed to create a most beautiful, delightful, small dog. Outcrosses to carefully chosen bloodlines stabilized the breed, resulting in the Coton we know today. Numerous of these small dogs moved to La Réunion and France when their owners emigrated from Madagascar. Some found their way to the US, where hardly anyone had ever heard of them before. Even on their native Madagascar, Cotons have remained a rarity.

The Maltese is the smallest of the Bichon breeds, recognized in most countries of the world today. Its coat is floor-length and straight, unlike that of the other Bichon breeds.

The Bolognese is the most similar of the Bichon breeds in looks to the Coton. This Bolognese has won many prizes in his native Italy.

What dog lover could resist the charms of the Coton de Tuléar? Ideal for children and adults alike, this breed possesses its own brand of pizzazz, marked with vitality and good humor.

COTON DE TULÉAR

PACKED WITH PERSONALITY

The Coton is a robust, charming small dog with a cheerful disposition. He will show everybody in the family just how much he loves them. The dog is always balanced and highly compatible with other members of his own breed. His hunting instincts, remnants of a time when the breed had to fend for itself, are still very much alive. It is said that Cotons had to hunt small wild animals in order to survive on their native Madagascar, and that they even formed small packs. This behavior is still obvious in the fact that they prefer to live in the company of a few animals of their own breed.

Signs of aggression are alien to him, and the fact that he is not a "yapper" makes his company pleasant. He appears to be always in a good mood and ever-ready for performing as a clown. He is a genuine harum-scarum, brimming with light-heartedness and energy. His small feet will carry him around with the swiftness of a weasel. A bundle of vitality, the little rascal will turn somersaults and show pirouettes.

Nonetheless, even with his clownish nature, the Coton is very intelligent and will make everybody his friend by learning readily and showing his mild-mannered disposition. With his surprising intelligence, he has the remarkable ability to intuitively detect the mood of his owner; if you are feeling down, you can be sure that your Coton will put you in a good mood with his humorous jester-like antics.

He is a perfect dog for apartment living, although he surely appreciates long walks. The Coton simply is a dog that adapts very well to his environment, whatever it may be. He will need to be groomed, and combing and brushing are tolerated with patience. He has a bubbly personality, but he keeps fairly quiet in the house. If left alone for some time out of necessity, he will look forward to

COTONS IN GERMANY
The Coton de Tuléar Club (CTC e.V.) in Germany was founded in 1982. The first litter (of six pups) was born in 1986 at the kennels of the CTC's founding member, Mrs. Göncz.

your return with elated anticipation. Being the miniature tornado he is, he will rush to welcome you with exuberance upon your return home. He is dynamite in a small package, not easily repressed; he is hardy and robust. This dog impresses all with his fantastic character, exuding happiness and harmony without end.

Bright and cheerful, the little Coton will jump into your arms or sit in front of you, wagging his tail, his black eyes sparkling from under the fringe of hair on his forehead. Or he may bounce across the yard on his hind legs, launching himself high into the air. If ignored, he will make his presence known with both elegance and enthusiasm: "Hello, I am here; I want to be stroked and cuddled!" Then it will be hard for

you to send him away. All in all, the Coton is an extremely lovable, affectionate housemate that considers himself an important member of your family…and he shows it! You will have a lot of trouble suppressing your smile at a dog that exudes so much pleasure and joy.

PHYSICAL CHARACTERISTICS
The Coton is a charming breed of small dog, weighing between about 4 kg (8.75 lb) and at maximum 6 kg (13.25 lb). Most remarkable are the breed's dark, round, vivid eyes that sparkle from under the long facial hair like two black jewels. This is a small bundle of fluff with both style and charm, seen most often in nearly pure white.

TEXTURE OF THE COAT AND COAT COLORS
The Coton's hair is long and soft, the white often interlaced with shades of biscuit, bluish-gray or brownish-gray. It is fairly lavish, like cotton, more fluffy than silky, and occasionally slightly wavy.

In 1994, Micky Ceriez, breeder and chairwoman of the Belgian Dog Club, explained in detail the workings of the Coton's colors. In her article in *Unser Kleinhund*, she wrote, "I have been breeding Cotons for many years. I bought my first Coton de Tuléar bitch in 1980 and she had her first litter in 1982. This stock went on to

---

DESCRIPTION BY DE FLACOURT

Etienne de Flacourt, a geographer and the governor of Fort Dauphin, described the Coton de Tuléar with these words: "There are a lot of small dogs with the long muzzle and short legs of a fox. Some are white. They have mated with the dogs brought from France, and they have stayed. They have short ears."

The Coton adapts to most situations, living contentedly in a home environment in the country or the city. A typical Coton is a happy dog who brings much pleasure and joy to all those around him.

produce many champions. During the course of many years of breeding, there were various opportunities to examine a large number of pups that were born with a large variety of colorations, ranging from pale champagne-colored ones right through to pure black. Many pups have color markings in their coats. In most of the cases these markings are situated on the head of the dog. But there have also been Cotons with specks of color on the body. These markings are no problem if they are not too numerous. With very light Cotons there was often a problem with missing pigmentation on the eyes, nose and paws. That was why I preferred further breeding those pups which had dark brown or black markings. Their pigmentation was just superior to that of pups born white."

Following is an explanation of the various colors:

White: Pups that are born pure white experience a color change towards pale yellow after a few days. These markings may remain forever or may even become slightly darker. Dogs like this will eventually be pale champagne-colored.

Ginger: This color is the least desirable. It will lighten only slightly with time and leave large dark ginger-colored markings (this is unsuitable as per the FCI breed standard).

Dark brown: Resulting from a mixture of dark brown and black hairs, this is my favorite color. It normally changes into almost white in mature specimens, but is actually a very pale yellow, visible only in bright sunlight or under strong artificial illumination. You should therefore check the undercoat of such pups; at an age of two months, when the pups are ready to leave their kennel, you will be able to recognize that these markings are becoming lighter.

Black: This is the most difficult color, as it can turn out to be the best if it later turns into a pure white or, conversely, the worst if it stays black or becomes gray. Black markings or a mixture of white and black hairs that produce gray spots, usually on the ears, are tolerated under the FCI standard as long as they do not destroy the overall appearance of a white dog. They are undesirable, however.

A breeder should not panic if his pups are born with spots, and a potential owner should realize that the coat color can change as the puppy grows. This section can

A MADAGASCAN FAVORITE
The Coton is highly favored by native Madagascans, as it still hunts vermin such as rats and mice. Local folk refer to the breed with affection as the "comedian" or "royal dog" even today.

Though usually seen in white, a range of colors exists in the Coton breed. The puppy color often changes as the dog matures to his eventual adult color.

be used as a reference to get an idea of what the various colors and markings may look like later in the pup's life. Also, do not forget that all of these rules have their exceptions!

GENDER DIFFERENCES

It is always advisable to make a decision about the gender of your dog before setting out to acquire one. The sex is obviously of much greater importance for a future breeder than for a pet owner. In principle, it can be stated that dogs and bitches do not differ substantially with regard to their nature. Both are equally friendly

and affectionate. With dogs being more dominant, though, they usually require a firmer hand than bitches.

Most bitches experience their first season (heat cycle) between six and ten months of age. From then on, unless the bitch is spayed, the seasonal cycles will occur every six months, with some variation being normal. A season usually lasts for about 21 days in total. The onset of a season is marked by a visible swelling of the vulva in conjunction with a discharge of bloody mucus. As the cycle progresses, the bloody discharge subsides, first becoming pale rosy and then clear. This is usually the case between days 10 and 15. This is also the best period of time if the bitch is to be mated.

If no mating is planned, you need to be extra careful during the bitch's heat cycle in preventing her from coming into contact with a male dog. Obviously, the bitch is now particularly attractive to any male dog. In order to prevent the bitch from being mated unintentionally, she should always be kept on leash during walks (for any dog's safety, male or female, the dog should always be on leash during walks, regardless of the time of year!). Pet shops offer protective "panties" that keep the bitch clean during her season, but these offer little protection from a determined male dog.

Male dogs usually mature between seven and nine months of age. They then also begin to delineate their territories with scent marks, which come in the form of a few drops of urine here and there. Once a young male dog begins to show this behavior, the owner should be conscientious about training his dog to not lift his leg wherever and whenever he wants to.

If you do not intend to breed or show your dog, neutering the male or spaying the female will eliminate pregnancy and certain

Colored ears add a bit of spice to the all-white Coton.

Viktoria Deak's kennel in Hungary produced this 6-month-old bitch, standing with an 18-month-old kennel-mate and a 5-year-old male.

health problems. In fact, responsible breeders will require owners of puppies destined for pet homes to neuter or spay at the appropriate age. One result of this is that the dog's metabolism slows down and the dog can become more prone to obesity. However, this undesirable side effect can easily be controlled by a balanced diet and regular exercise. Plus, the positive outcomes of neutering and spaying, including health benefits such as eliminating or reducing the risk of certain types of cancers in both genders, outweigh this easily avoided negative.

HORMONE SUPPRESSION

There are a number of products available that suppress or reduce the production of hormones in both bitches and dogs, commonly referred to as anti-androgens. Their action is limited to a very short period of time, and side effects may be experienced. They should therefore only be used under the supervision of an experienced veterinarian.

THE COTON WITH CHILDREN

It is always a pleasurable experience to see that children meet animals with a display of natural, unprejudiced trust. Children just seem to love petting and playing with animals…and kids most often wish for a dog as a companion. Parents must be conscious of their responsibility, toward both their children and the new canine member of the family, if they eventually give in to their kids' begging and take in a little four-legged companion. The children must be made to understand that a dog is everything but another toy, that the dog is a living being that needs love and feels pain just like they do. The children also must be taught that a dog needs structure and periods of rest in his day-to-day life.

The entire family must be aware of the fact that this little clumsy ball of fluff will soon turn into a full-grown dog, and that the dog's need for care, love and attention is something that lasts from puppyhood throughout his entire life. The children in the household should therefore be entrusted with smaller tasks, such as feeding, brushing and taking the dog for walks. Which tasks they are able to perform depends on their individual ages, and they should taught each task step-by-step by the adults. The proper approach to all matters pertaining to the dog teaches the children important lessons for their own lives as well, which shows that consideration and empathy can be learned through play. What must be avoided, on the other hand, is that the necessary assignments turn into disdained chores.

POTENTIAL BAD HABITS IN THE COTON

Every single breed of dog can develop bad habits as well as good ones, and the former may not be what we as owners find tolerable. For example, despite his short legs, the Coton is very much able to jump up and play on chairs and upholstered furniture. Even low tables may be scaled with considerable skill. Normally, the dog will have his own "furniture" in the form of a crate, basket or dog bed, and he needs to be taught, without any misunderstanding, what his domain is.

Verbal scolding (firm, not yelling) or clapping your hands may be all that is required to call him to order. If this does not help, more drastic measures may be necessary. For example, if your intention is to keep your Coton from jumping on a chair, you can seize him by the ruff the moment he jumps up. Holding him up, you would then scold him with a

very firm "No." The moment he tries to repeat his mistake, you would repeat the same procedure until he eventually associates his behavior with the punishment that follows, and therefore stops the undesirable behavior. Likewise, praise is always in order for proper behavior.

Another bad habit in the Coton is his tendency to beg for food. It cannot be emphasized enough that constant nibbling is the major cause of obesity in dogs and can lead to severe health problems. Don't let your Coton's pleading eyes cause you to lose your resolve...do not "reward" him with food when he begs, as this will make him think that begging is good behavior. Make sure that everyone in the family knows and follows this rule.

There is no greater experience than watching a child and a Coton meet for the first time. This is a display of mutual, loving trust. Dogs don't lie about love.

THE SECRET TO HAPPINESS?

In France, the Coton de Tuléar has been referred to as an "anti-depressant," as the breed is particularly suitable for people suffering from frequent bouts of sadness, melancholy and depression. This little jester restores happiness in his owner over and over again.

COTON DE TULÉAR

WHAT IS A BREED STANDARD?

A breed standard is a written document, approved by a kennel club or breed club, that details the dog's physical characteristics, temperament and abilities necessary for its intended original purpose. In other words, what makes this breed what it is? What sets it apart from every other breed? Standards are written by knowledgeable dog experts who hope to ensure the quality of a particular breed for future generations. Without such guidelines, specific inherent breed characteristics may be altered or completely eliminated over time.

By putting down in words all of the necessary and desirable characteristics of a breed, and thus the ideal representative of that breed, the standard becomes a "blueprint" or "roadmap" of sorts. Standards are used by breeders to assist them in breeding toward the elusive goal of perfection. While no dog is absolutely perfect, the dogs that adhere closest to the ideal are what breeders will determine is show or breeding stock. That being said, the standard is also used by dog-show judges to compare actual dogs to the ideal. The dog that the judge feels adheres closest to the ideal is the winner of the class, and so on down the line as the classes progress to Best in Show.

WHAT IS THE FCI?

Established in 1911, the Fédération Cynologique Internationale (FCI) represents the "world kennel club." This interna-

CLUB CONTACTS

You can get information about dog shows from the national kennel clubs:

Fédération Cynologique Internationale
14, rue Leopold II, B-6530 Thuin, Belgium
www.fci.be

United Kennel Club
100 E. Kilgore Road, Kalamazoo, MI 49002
www.ukcdogs.com

Canadian Kennel Club
89 Skyway Ave., Suite 100, Etobicoke, Ontario
M9W 6R4 Canada
www.ckc.ca

American Rare Breed Association
9921 Frank Tippett Road
Cheltenham, MD 20623
www.arba.org

tional body brings uniformity to the breeding, judging and showing of pure-bred dogs. Although the FCI originally included only five European nations: France, Germany, Austria, the Netherlands and Belgium (which remains its headquarters), the organization today embraces nations on six continents and recognizes well over 300 breeds of pure-bred dog.

The FCI sponsors both national and international shows. The hosting country determines the judging system, and breed standards are always based on the breed's country of origin. Dogs from every country can participate in these impressive canine spectacles, the largest of which is the World Dog Show, hosted in a different country each year.

There are three titles attainable through the FCI: the International Champion, which is the most prestigious; the International Beauty Champion, which is based on aptitude certificates in different countries; and the International Trial Champion, which is based on achievement in obedience trials in different countries.

An FCI title requires a dog to win three CACs (*Certificats d'Aptitude au Championnat*), at regional or club shows under three different judges who are breed specialists. The title of International Champion is gained by winning four CACIBs

FCI INFORMATION

There are 330 breeds recognized by the FCI, and each breed is considered to be "owned" by a specific country. Each breed standard is a cooperative effort between the breed's country and the FCI's Standards and Scientific Commissions. Judges use these official breed standards at shows held in FCI member countries. One of the functions of the FCI is to update and translate the breed standards into French, English, Spanish and German.

(*Certificats d'Aptitude au Championnat International de Beauté*), which are offered only at international shows, with at least a one-year lapse between the first and fourth award.

The FCI is divided into ten groups, of which the Coton de

A troop of Cotons, competing at the World Dog Show, the most prestigious of the FCI's dog shows. The breed is fast becoming an international favorite.

TEN GROUPS

FCI-recognized breeds are divided into ten groups:

Group 1: Sheepdogs and Cattledogs (except Swiss Cattledogs)

Group 2: Pinschers and Schnauzers, Molossians, Swiss Mountain Dogs and Swiss Cattledogs

Group 3: Terriers

Group 4: Dachshunds

Group 5: Spitz- and primitive-type dogs

Group 6: Scenthounds and related breeds

Group 7: Pointing dogs

Group 8: Retrievers, Flushing dogs and Water dogs

Group 9: Companion and Toy dogs

Group 10: Sighthounds

Tuléar is a member of Group 9, Companion and Toy Dogs. At the World Dog Show, the following classes are offered for each breed: Puppy Class (6–9 months), Junior Class (9–18 months), Open Class (15 months or older) and Champion Class. A dog can be awarded a classification of Excellent, Very Good, Good, Sufficient and Not Sufficient. Puppies can be awarded classifications of Very Promising, Promising or Not Promising. Four placements are made in each class. After all classes are judged, a Best of Breed is selected. Other special groups and classes may also be shown. Each exhibitor showing a dog receives a written evaluation from the judge.

Besides the World Dog Show, the European Champions Show and other all-breed shows, the Coton de Tuléar can be exhibited and participate in specialty shows held by the breed clubs in different countries. Specialty shows may have their own regulations from country to country.

Following is a translation of the breed standard for the Coton de Tuléar as approved by the FCI. The breed is recognized as one of Madagascan origin, but the standard was developed in France.

THE FCI STANDARD FOR THE COTON DE TULÉAR

TRANSLATION
Pamela Jeans-Brown, Renée Sporre-Willes, Raymond Triquet.

ORIGIN
Madagascar.

PATRONAGE
France.

DATE OF PUBLICATION OF THE ORIGINAL VALID STANDARD
November 25, 1999.

UTILIZATION
Companion dog.

FCI CLASSIFICATION

Group 9, Companion and Toy Dogs. Section 1.2, Coton de Tuléar. Without working trial.

BRIEF HISTORICAL SUMMARY

Introduced to France long before its official recognition in 1970, this newcomer from Madagascar quickly acquired a prominent position among the companion dogs of this country; today it is widespread all over the world.

GENERAL APPEARANCE

Small, long-haired companion dog with a white cotton-textured coat, with round, dark eyes and a lively, intelligent expression.

IMPORTANT PROPORTIONS

- The height at the withers in relationship to the length of the body is 2 to 3.
- The length of the head in relationship to the length of the body is 2 to 5.

The Coton de Tuléar possesses a soft and supple coat on a properly proportioned body. The standard describes the ideal dog in detail.

SHOW-QUALITY SHOWS

While you may purchase a puppy in the hope of having a successful career in the show ring, it is impossible to tell, at eight to ten weeks of age, whether your dog will be a contender. Some promising pups end up with minor to serious faults that prevent them from taking home an award, but this certainly does not mean they can't be the best of companions for you and your family. To find out if your potential show dog is show-quality, enter him in a match to see how a judge evaluates him. You may also take him back to your breeder as he matures to see what he might advise.

- The length of the skull in relationship to that of the muzzle is 9 to 5.

BEHAVIOR/TEMPERAMENT:
Of a happy temperament, stable, very sociable with humans and other dogs; it adapts perfectly to all ways of life. The temperament of the Coton is one of the main characteristics of the breed.

HEAD
Short, seen from above triangular.

CRANIAL REGION
Skull: Seen from the front slightly rounded; rather wide in relation to its length. Superciliary arches only slightly developed. Slight frontal groove. Occipital protuberance and crest only slightly accentuated. Well developed zygomatic arches. Stop: Slight.

FACIAL REGION
Nose: In the extension of the nasal bridge; black; brown is tolerated; nostrils wide open. Muzzle: Straight. Lips: Fine, tight, of the same color as the nose. Jaws/Teeth: Teeth well aligned. Scissors bite, pincer bite or inverted bite without losing contact. The absence of PM1s is not penalized; the M3s are not taken into consideration. Cheeks: Lean. Eyes: Rather rounded, dark, lively, wide apart; the rims of the eyelids are well pigmented with black or brown according to the

color of the nose. Ears: Pendulous, triangular, set high on the skull, fine at the tips; carried close to the cheeks, reaching the corners of the lips. Covered with white hairs or with some traces of light gray (mixture of white and black hairs giving a light gray appearance) or red-roan (mixture of white and fawn hairs giving a red-roan appearance—lemon).

NECK
Well muscled, slightly arched. Neck well set into shoulders. Proportion of neck to body 1 to 5. Clean neck with no dewlap.

BODY
Topline very slightly convex. Dog longer than high. Withers: Only slightly pronounced. Back and loin: Strong back, topline very slightly arched. Loin well muscled. Croup: Oblique, short and muscled. Chest: Well developed, well let down to elbow level, long. Ribs well sprung. Belly: Tucked up but not excessively.

THE OVERALL STRUCTURE
The overall structure of the FCI is divided into several bodies:
—General Assembly
—Executive Committee and General Committee
—Compulsory Commissions (Standards, Scientific and Legal)
—Non-compulsory Commissions

TAIL
Low set, in the axis of the spinal column. At rest, carried below the hock, the tip being raised. On the move, carried gaily curved over the back, with the point towards the nape, the withers, the back or the loin. In dog with abundant coat, the tip may rest on the dorsal-lumbar region.

LIMBS
Forequarters: The front legs are upright. Shoulder and upper arms: Oblique shoulder, muscled. Scapulo-humeral angle about 120° The length of the upper arm bone corresponds approximately to that of the shoulder blade. Lower arm: Humero-radial angle about 120°. Lower arms vertical and parallel; well muscled, with good bone. The length of the lower arm corresponds approximately to that of the upper arm. Carpus (Pastern joint): A continuation of the line of the lower arm. Metacarpus (Pastern): Strong, seen in profile, sloping very slightly. Forefeet: Small, round toes tight, arched; pads pigmented.
Hindquarters: The hindlegs are upright. Though dewclaws are not sought, their presence is not penalized. Upper thigh: Strongly muscled; coxo-femoral angle about 80°. Lower thigh: Oblique, forming with the femur an angle of about 120°. Hock joint: Dry, well defined, angle of the hock about 160°. Metatarsus (Rear

TEMPERAMENT PLUS

Although it seems that physical conformation is the only factor considered in the show ring, temperament is also of utmost importance. An aggressive or fearful dog should not be shown, as bad behavior will not be tolerated and may pose a threat to the judge, other exhibitors, you and your dog.

pastern): Vertical. Hindfeet: Similar to forefeet.

GAIT/MOVEMENT

Free and flowing, without covering a lot of ground; topline retained on the move. No sign of uneven movement.

SKIN

Fine, stretched tight over all the body; although of pink color, it can be pigmented.

COAT

Hair: This is one of the main characteristics of the breed from which its very name derives. Very soft and supple, with the texture of cotton, never hard or rough, the coat is dense, profuse and can be very slightly wavy.
Color: Ground color: White. A few slight shadings of light gray color (mixture of white and black hairs) or of red-roan (mixture of white and fawn hairs) are permitted on the ears. On other parts of the

body, such shadings can be tolerated if they do not alter the general appearance of a white coat. They are however not sought after.

SIZE AND WEIGHT

Height at withers: Males: 26 to 28 cm, tolerance of 2 cm above and 1 cm below. Bitches: 23 to 25 cm, tolerance of 2 cm above and 1 cm below.
Weight: Males: From 4 kg to a maximum of 6 kg. Bitches: From 3.5 kg to a maximum of 5 kg.

FAULTS

Any departure from the foregoing points should be considered a fault and the seriousness with which the fault should be regarded should be in exact proportion to its degree.

Serious Faults:
- Skull: Flat or too domed; narrow.
- Muzzle: Disproportion between skull and muzzle.
- Eyes: Light; too almond-shaped; entropion, ectropion; prominent eyes.
- Ears: Too short; with insufficiently length of hair; ears folding backward (rose ear).
- Neck: Too short, too stuffy in shoulders, too slender.
- Topline: Too arched, sway back.
- Croup: Horizontal, narrow.
- Shoulders: Straight.
- Limbs: Turned inward or

A lovely two-year-old bitch named D'Elete la Palma, owned by Viktoria Deak.

The main reason that standards exist is to protect the desired type of the breed. Pure-bred dogs should have puppies with predictable characteristics as to size, color and other physical characteristics, as well as temperament and personality traits.

outward; out at elbows; hocks wide set or too close; straight angulation.

- Coat: Too short, too wavy, curly.
- Pigmentation: Partially lacking or too light pigmentation of eyelids or lips; discolored nose, with unpigmented areas.

Eliminating Faults:

General type:

- Lack of type (insufficient breed characteristics, which means that the animal on the whole does not sufficiently resemble other examples of the breed).
- Size and weight outside the requirements and tolerance of the standard.

Particular points:

- Foreface: Bridge of nose convex.
- Eyes: Bulging, with signs of dwarfism; too light; wall eyes.
- Ears: Pricked or semi-pricked.
- Tail: Not reaching to hock; high set; completely curled (forming a tight ring); carried flat on the back or against the thighs; carried candle-like; tailless.
- Coat: Atypical, tightly curled, woolly, silky.
- Color: Heavily marked; any marking of a definite black.
- Pigmentation: Total lack of pigment on eye rims, nose or lips.

Anomalies:

- Overshot or undershot mouth with lack of contact between the incisors; vertical gaping of the incisors.
- Absence of teeth other than the PM1s or the M3s.
- Aggressive or extremely shy specimens.

N.B.: Male animals should have two apparently normal testicles that have fully descended into the scrotum.

PRACTICE AT HOME

If you have decided to show your dog, you must train him to gait around the ring by your side at the correct pace and pattern, and to tolerate being handled and examined by the judge. Most breeds require complete dentition, all breeds require a particular bite (scissors, level or undershot) and all males must have two apparently normal testicles fully descended into the scrotum. Enlist family and friends to hold mock trials in your yard to prepare your future champion.

Choosing a Coton should be a family affair! If you want a Coton puppy for your family, be sure everyone is involved in the selection process.

COTON DE TULÉAR

WHERE TO BEGIN

If you are convinced that the Coton de Tuléar is the ideal dog for you, and you and your family are ready to add one to your family, it's time to learn about where to find a puppy and what to look for. Locating a litter of Cotons may be somewhat of a challenge for the new owner, as this is a rare breed in most parts of the world. Nonetheless, there is sufficient interest in the breed wherever it is found. You will be able to find contacts within the breed who can help you locate reputable breeders in your country. Remember that, when choosing a breeder, reputation is much more important than convenience of location.

Choosing a breeder is an important first step in dog ownership. Fortunately, the majority of Coton breeders is devoted to the breed and its well-being. Clubs devoted solely to the Coton de Tuléar, as well as kennel clubs with which the breed is registered and perhaps all-breed clubs, can point you in the right direction.

PEDIGREE VS. REGISTRATION CERTIFICATE

Too often new owners are confused between these two important documents. Your puppy's pedigree, essentially a family tree, is a written record of a dog's genealogy of three generations or more. The pedigree will show you the names as well as performance titles of all dogs in your pup's background. Your breeder must provide you with a registration application, with his part properly filled out. You must complete the application and send it to the AKC with the proper fee. Every puppy must come from a litter that has been AKC-registered by the breeder, born in the USA and from a sire and dam that are also registered with the AKC.

The seller must provide you with complete records to identify the puppy. The AKC requires that the seller provide the buyer with the following: breed; sex, color and markings; date of birth; litter number (when available); names and registration numbers of the parents; breeder's name; and date sold or delivered.

Potential owners are encouraged to attend dog shows or trials at which there are Cotons participating. In the US, Cotons compete in conformation and other events run by the American Rare Breed Association (ARBA), the States Kennel Club (SKC) and the United Kennel Club (UKC), as well as at specialty shows held by certain breed clubs. You may not be looking for a show dog, but shows will give you a chance to see the Cotons in action, to meet the owners and handlers firsthand and to get an idea of what Cotons look like outside a photographer's lens.

With a companion breed like the Coton, personality is just as important as physical characteristics, soundness and good health. A sweet puppy who approaches you is certainly a good start.

PUPPY APPEARANCE
Your puppy should have a well-fed appearance but not a distended abdomen, which may indicate worms or incorrect feeding, or both. The body should be firm, with a solid feel. The skin of the abdomen should be pale pink and clean, without signs of scratching or rash. Check the hind legs to see if the breeder has had the dewclaws removed.

Provided you approach the handlers when they are not busy with the dogs, most are more than willing to answer questions, recommend breeders and give advice.

Once you have contacted and met a breeder or two and made your choice about which breeder is best suited to your needs, it's time to visit the litter. If the breeder is not located within feasible traveling distance, he should be able to send you videos of the pups and parents, and will conduct the interview process by phone. Keep in mind that many top breeders have waiting lists, especially with rare breeds. Sometimes new owners have to wait a year or more for a puppy. If you are really committed to the breeder whom you've selected, then you will wait (and hope for an early arrival!). If not, you may need to seek out another breeder with whom you are comfortable. Don't be too anxious, however. If the breeder doesn't have a waiting list, there is probably a good reason. It's no different than visiting a restaurant with no clientele. The better restaurants always have waiting lists—and it's usually worth the wait. Besides, isn't a puppy more important than a nice meal?

Since you are likely to be choosing a Coton as a pet dog and not a show dog, you simply should select a pup that is friendly, attractive and healthy. The breeder should have performed all of the necessary health screenings on the parents to ensure that hereditary problems are not passed on to the puppies, and he should provide you with the appropriate documentation. The Coton is affected by certain eye problems, and patellar luxation (dislocating kneecaps) is common in many small breeds. Dogs affected by these or other genetic disorders should never be bred. All puppies in the litter should appear healthy, with clear eyes, healthy coats, clean ears, fresh-smelling breath and no indication of diarrhea.

Breeders commonly allow visitors to see their litters by around the fifth or sixth week, and puppies leave for their new homes between the eighth and

BOY OR GIRL?
An important consideration to be discussed is the sex of your puppy. For a family companion, a bitch may be the better choice, considering the female's inbred concern for all young creatures and her accompanying tolerance and patience. It is always advisable to spay a pet bitch or neuter a pet male, which may guarantee your dog a longer life.

tenth weeks, although some breeders keep Coton puppies even longer. Breeders who permit their puppies to leave early are more interested in making a profit than in their puppies' well-being, and these breeders are to be avoided. Puppies need to learn the rules of the pack from their dams, and most dams continue teaching the pups manners and dos and don'ts until at least around the

When you find a conscientious, knowledgeable breeder, you will know it by the quality of the puppies. Properly bred Cotons glisten with personality, purity and good health.

THE COTON LITTER

Like with most small breeds of dog, there is great variation in the size of Coton litters. Although the Coton de Tuléar is a small breed, it is also a fairly robust animal. An average litter obtained from a healthy bitch comprises four to five pups on the average, though it is possible to find litters of six or more pups (although more than six is rare).

A factor of substantial influence is the day on which the mating takes place. Is it the peak of the bitch's season? The time at which the mating occurs may very well determine how many eggs are available for fertilization in the bitch and how many sperm cells the male dog can provide. Young breeding bitches usually have larger litters than older females,

eighth week. Breeders spend significant amounts of time with the Coton toddlers so that the pups are able to interact with the "other species," i.e. humans. Given the long history that dogs and humans have, bonding between the two species is natural but must be nurtured. A well-bred, well-socialized Coton pup wants nothing more than to be near you and please you.

TEMPERAMENT COUNTS
Your selection of a good puppy can be determined by your needs. A show potential or a good pet? It is your choice. Every puppy, however, should be of good temperament. Although show-quality puppies are bred and raised with emphasis on physical conformation, responsible breeders strive for equally good temperament. Do not buy from a breeder who concentrates solely on physical beauty at the expense of personality.

although this is by no means a rule to rely on. Another aspect that can determine litter size is the overall condition of the breeding bitch.

A personal note may be appropriate here: A breeder should not judge the quality of a breeding bitch on the basis of the sizes of her litters alone. It is far more important that she produces healthy pups and then raises them confidently without artificial aids. It is also of utmost importance that the bitch is able to recover physically and psychologically between her individual litters. For this reason, there should be a span of at least two years between litters.

The Coton is no kennel dog, and pups should not be raised separately from their mother until they leave for new homes. Pups raised in a kennel environment, without their dam, are deprived of exploring their surroundings, of becoming used to changes around them, of experiencing environmental influences and new sights and sounds, of learning the rules that their mother will teach them; they basically only get to know their particular area of confinement. They will not know a tree, grass, birds or the normal sounds and activity of a household. In order for them to become alert pups that are happy to make new contacts, they should be raised as part of their extended family, where they can be in touch with everything that goes on in daily life.

THE DEVELOPING COTON PUP

It takes about two years for a mop of hair that leaves the kennel weighing about 1500 grams (about 3.25 lb) to turn into a mature "cotton dog," a Coton de Tuléar. During this period of time, the youngster

TIME TO GO HOME
Breeders rarely release puppies until they are eight to ten weeks of age. This is an acceptable age for most breeds of dog, excepting toy breeds, which are sometimes held until around 12 weeks, given their petite sizes. If a breeder has a puppy that is 12 weeks of age or older, it is likely well socialized and has begun to be house-trained. Be sure that the puppy is otherwise healthy before deciding to take him home.

Part of the socialization process includes allowing the pup to explore the world around him. An ex-pen is a great tool to help confine your pup while he is in new surroundings.

passes through various phases that are marked by changes in his physical features and character. The smaller a dog is, the faster he will have grow to his full size. The initially fluffy baby coat is replaced almost imperceptibly from about five months of age by the heavier, more cotton-like adult coat; any dark markings usually also disappear in this process.

This is also the time when the pup loses his baby teeth and his adult teeth come in, typically beginning with the upper and lower incisors and followed by the teeth farther back. The adult teeth should all be in place at about nine months of age. Should the milk (baby) teeth still be present at age 12 months, they should be removed by a veterinarian to prevent them from interfering with the formation of a correct bite. Provided with adequate care, the coat should grow to a decent length and be of a good texture by the end of the dog's first year of life. In the case of a show

ARE YOU PREPARED?

Unfortunately, when a puppy is bought by someone who does not take into consideration the time and attention that dog ownership requires, it is the puppy who suffers when he is either abandoned or placed in a shelter by a frustrated owner. So all of the "homework" you do in preparation for your pup's arrival will benefit you both. The more informed you are, the more you will know what to expect and the better equipped you will be to handle the ups and downs of raising a puppy. Hopefully, everyone in the household is willing to do his part in raising and caring for the pup. The anticipation of owning a dog often brings a lot of promises from excited family members: "I will walk him every day," "I will feed him," "I will house-train him," etc., but these things take time and effort, and promises can easily be forgotten once the novelty of the new pet has worn off.

dog, it now becomes time to pay special attention to the dog's preparation for the show ring.

The nature of your Coton will also change as he grows up. The oh-so-cute, playful and "easy-to-care-for" pup that was effortlessly integrated into your daily routines will now suddenly present himself as willful and occasionally even stubborn. In this regard, there seems to be not much of a difference between male dogs and bitches. The young dog with "leadership qualities" in particular will, from time to time, test his position in the family hierarchy to see if he can move up in rank. This makes it imperative for you to shape your dog's behavior with a firm, but still kind and loving, hand. The more consistent and diligent you are during this time, the sooner the dog will be convinced that it is you who calls the shots and that good manners make life easier.

COMMITMENT OF OWNERSHIP

After considering all of these factors, you have most likely already made some very important decisions about selecting your puppy. You have chosen the Coton de Tuléar, which means that you have decided that the breed possesses the characteristics you want in a dog and that this type of dog will best fit into your family and lifestyle. If you have selected a breeder, you have gone a step further—you have done your research and found a responsible, conscientious person who breeds quality Cotons and who should be a reliable source of help as you and your puppy adjust to life

"YOU BETTER SHOP AROUND!"

Finding a reputable breeder who sells healthy pups is very important, but make sure that the breeder you choose is not only someone you respect but also someone with whom you feel comfortable. Your breeder will be a resource long after you buy your puppy, and you must be able to call with reasonable questions without being made to feel like a pest! If you don't connect on a personal level, investigate some other breeders before making a final decision.

FEEDING TIPS

You will probably start feeding your pup the same food that he has been getting from the breeder; the breeder should give you a few days' supply to start you off. Although you should not give your pup too many treats, you will want to have puppy treats on hand for coaxing, training, rewards, etc. Be careful, though, as a small pup's calorie requirements are relatively low and a few treats can add up to almost a full day's worth of calories without the required nutrition.

together. If you have observed a litter in action, you have obtained a firsthand look at the dynamics of a puppy "pack" and, thus, you have learned about each pup's individual personality—perhaps you have even found one that particularly appeals to you.

However, even if you have not yet found the Coton puppy of your dreams, observing pups when you have the chance will help you learn to recognize certain behavior and to determine what a pup's behavior indicates about his temperament. You will be able to pick out which pups are the leaders, which ones are less outgoing, which ones are confident, shy, playful, friendly, aggressive, etc. Equally as important, you will learn to recognize what a healthy pup should look and act like. All of these things will help you in your search, and when you find the Coton that was meant for you, you will know it!

Researching your breed, selecting a responsible breeder and observing as many pups as possible are all important steps on the way to dog ownership. It may seem like a lot of effort... and you have not even taken the pup home yet! Remember, though, you cannot be too careful when it comes to deciding on the type of dog you want and

HANDLE WITH CARE

You should be extremely careful about handling tiny puppies. Not that you might hurt them, but that the pups' mother may exhibit what is called "maternal aggression." It is a natural, instinctive reaction for the dam to protect her young against anything she interprets as predatory or possibly harmful to her pups. The sweetest, most gentle of bitches, after whelping a litter, often reacts this way, even to her owner.

finding out about your prospective pup's background. Buying a puppy is not—or *should* not be—just another whimsical purchase. This is one instance in which you actually do get to choose your own family!

You may be thinking that buying a puppy should be fun—it should not be so serious and so much work. Keep in mind that your puppy is not a cuddly stuffed toy or decorative lawn ornament; rather, he is a living creature that will become a real member of your family. You will come to realize that, while buying a puppy is a pleasurable and exciting endeavor, it is not something to be taken lightly. Relax...the fun will start when the pup comes home!

Always keep in mind that a puppy is nothing more than a baby in a fluffy disguise...a baby who is virtually helpless in a human world and who trusts his owner for fulfillment of his basic needs for survival. In addition to food, water and shelter, your pup needs care, protection, guidance and love. If you are not prepared to commit

Here is a baby in a furry disguise, and quite a good one!

Consider adopting an adult Coton if you don't have the time to raise a puppy. Discuss this possibility with your breeder. Many times breeders have retired show or breeding dogs that need to find good homes.

to this, then you are not prepared to own a dog.

"Wait a minute," you say. "How hard could this be? All of my neighbors own dogs and they seem to be doing just fine. Why should I have to worry about all of this?" Well, you should not worry about it; in fact, you will probably find that once your Coton pup gets used to his new home, he will fall into his place in the family quite naturally. However, it never hurts to emphasize the

YOUR SCHEDULE . . .
If you lead an erratic, unpredictable life, with daily or weekly changes in your work requirements, consider the problems of owning a puppy. The new puppy has to be fed regularly, social-ized (loved, petted, handled, intro-duced to other people) and, most importantly, allowed to go outdoors for house-training. As the dog gets older, he can be more tolerant of deviations in his feeding and relief schedule.

commitment of dog ownership. With some time and patience, it is really not too difficult to raise a curious and exuberant Coton de Tuléar pup to be a well-adjusted and well-mannered adult dog—a dog that could be your most loyal friend.

PREPARING PUPPY'S PLACE IN YOUR HOME
Researching your breed and finding a breeder are only two aspects of the "homework" you will have to do before bringing a Coton puppy into your home. You will also have to prepare your home and family for the new addition. Much as you would prepare a nursery for a newborn baby, you will need to designate a place in your home that will be the puppy's own. How you prepare your home will depend on how much free-

dom the dog will be allowed. Will he be allowed full run of the house or will certain rooms be off-limits? Whatever you decide, you must ensure that the pup has a place that he can call his own.

When you bring your new puppy into your home, you are bringing him into what will become his home as well. Obviously, you did not buy a puppy with the intentions of catering to his every whim and allowing him to "rule the roost," but in order for a puppy to grow into a stable, well-adjusted dog, he has to feel comfortable in his surroundings. Remember, he is leaving the warmth and security of his mother and littermates, as well as the familiarity of the only place he has ever known, so it is important to make his transition as easy as possible. By preparing a place in your home for the puppy, you are making him feel as welcome as possible in a strange new place. It should not take him long to get used to it, but the sudden shock of being transplanted is somewhat traumatic for a young pup. Imagine how a small child would feel in the same situation—that is how your puppy must be feeling. It is up to you to reassure him and to let him know, "Little cotton dog, you are going to like it here!"

PUPPY PERSONALITY
When a litter becomes available to you, choosing a pup out of all those adorable faces will not be an easy task! Sound temperament is of utmost importance, but each pup has his own personality and some may be better suited to you than others. A feisty, independent pup will do well in a home with older children and adults, while quiet, shy puppies will thrive in homes with minimal noise and distractions. Your breeder knows the pups best and should be able to guide you in the right direction.

WHAT YOU SHOULD BUY

CRATE

To someone unfamiliar with the use of crates in dog training, it may seem like punishment to shut a dog in a crate, but this is not the case at all. More and more breeders and trainers are recommending crates as

PHOTO COURTESY OF DOSKOCIL

or when he just needs a break. Many dogs sleep in their crates overnight. With soft bedding and his favorite toy, a crate becomes a cozy pseudo-den for your dog. Like his ancestors, he too will seek out the comfort and retreat of a den—you just happen to be providing him with something a little more luxurious than what his early ancestors enjoyed.

As far as purchasing a crate, the type that you buy is up to you. It will most likely be one of the two most popular types: wire or fiberglass. There are advantages and disadvantages to each type. For example, a wire crate is more open, allowing the air to flow through and affording the dog a view of what is going on around him, while a fiberglass crate is sturdier. Both can double as travel crates, providing protection for the dog in the car, although a fiberglass crate is required for air travel. The size of the crate is another thing to consider. Puppies do not stay puppies forever but, fortunately for Coton owners, they do not grow to be too big. Therefore, it will be easy to select a crate that will suit the Coton both in puppyhood and in adulthood. A full-grown Coton can stand up to 12 inches high at the shoulder, depending on gender and individual development, so keep this in mind

preferred tools for pet puppies as well as show puppies. Crates are not cruel—crates have many humane and highly effective uses in dog care and training. For example, crate training is a popular and very successful house-training method. In addition, a crate can keep your dog safe during travel and, perhaps most importantly, a crate provides your dog with a place of his own in your home. It serves as a "doggie bedroom" of sorts—your Coton can curl up in his crate when he wants to sleep

when selecting a crate that will comfortably house your dog.

BEDDING

A soft crate pad and perhaps a cuddly blanket in the dog's crate will help the dog feel more at home. First, these things will take the place of the leaves, twigs, etc., that the pup would use in the wild to make a den; the pup can make his own "burrow" in the crate. Although your pup is far removed from his den-making ancestors, the denning instinct is still a part of his genetic makeup. Second, until you take your pup home, he has been sleeping amid the warmth of his mother and litter-

The most valuable tool you will purchase for your Coton is his crate. Not only does the crate facilitate house-training but it also teaches the dog good manners, clean habits and structure, which are needed for the dog's whole life.

mates, and while a blanket is not the same as a warm, breathing body, it still provides heat and something with which to snuggle. You will want to wash your pup's bedding frequently in case he has a potty accident in his crate, and replace or remove any padding or blanket that becomes ragged and starts to fall apart.

Toys

Toys are a must for dogs of all ages, especially for curious playful pups. Puppies are the "children" of the dog world, and what child does not love toys? Chew toys provide enjoyment for both dog and owner—your dog will enjoy playing with his favorite toys, while you will enjoy the fact that they distract him from chewing on your expensive shoes and leather sofa. Puppies love to chew; in

Introduce the puppy to his crate on the first day. Breeders often start the crate-training process by allowing the pups to sleep in crates before they are released to their new homes.

CRATE-TRAINING TIPS

During crate training, you can partition off the section of the crate in which the pup stays. If he is given too big an area, this will hinder your training efforts. Crate training is based on the fact that a dog does not like to soil his sleeping quarters, so it is ineffective to keep a pup in an area that is so big that he can eliminate in one end and get far enough away from it to sleep. Also, you want to make the crate den-like for the pup. Blankets and a favorite toy will make the crate cozy for the small pup; as he grows, you may want to evict some of his "roommates" to make more room. It will take some coaxing at first, but be patient. Given some time to get used to it, your pup will adapt to his new home-within-a-home quite nicely.

---

fact, chewing is a physical need for pups as they are teething, and everything looks appetizing! The full range of your possessions—from old slippers to Oriental carpet—are fair game in the eyes of a teething pup. Puppies are not all that discerning when it comes to finding something literally to "sink their teeth into"—everything tastes great!

Only durable chew toys made for dogs should be offered to your Coton. Toys such as sturdy nylon bones and well-made rope toys are designed to last, and do not have pieces that could break off. Dog toys are made in different sizes for different breeds, so purchase toys made for smaller dogs, making sure that they are not small enough for the dog to swallow.

Breeders advise owners to resist stuffed toys, because they can become de-stuffed in no time. The overly excited pup may ingest the stuffing, which is neither nutritious nor digestible. Similarly, squeaky toys are quite popular, but must be avoided unless you are able to supervise. Perhaps a squeaky toy can be used as an aid in training, but not for free play. If a pup "disembowels" one of these, the small plastic squeaker inside can be dangerous if swallowed.

Monitor the condition of all your pup's toys carefully and get rid of any that have been chewed to the point of becoming potentially dangerous. Be careful of natural bones, which have a tendency to splinter into sharp, dangerous pieces. Also be careful of rawhide, which can turn into pieces that are easy to swallow and become a mushy mess on your carpet.

LEAD

A nylon lead is probably the best option, as it is the most resistant to puppy teeth should your pup take a liking to chewing on his lead. Of course, this

TOYS, TOYS, TOYS!

With a big variety of dog toys available, and so many that look like they would be a lot of fun for a dog, be careful in your selection. It is amazing what a set of puppy teeth can do to an innocent-looking toy, so, obviously, safety is a major consideration. Be sure to choose the most durable products that you can find. Hard nylon bones and toys are a safe bet, and many of them are offered in different scents and flavors that will be sure to capture your dog's attention. It is always fun to play a game of fetch with your dog, and there are balls and flying discs that are specially made to withstand dog teeth.

Your local pet shop will have a large variety of leads from which you may choose one that best suits your needs. The Coton can do very well with a light nylon lead.

is a habit that should be nipped in the bud, but, if your pup likes to chew on his lead, he has a very slim chance of being able to chew through the strong nylon. Nylon leads are also lightweight, which is good for a young Coton who is just getting used to the idea of walking on a lead. For everyday walking and safety purposes, the nylon lead is a good choice.

As your pup grows up and gets used to walking on the lead, and can do it politely, you may want to purchase a flexible lead. These leads allow you to extend the length to give the dog a broader area to explore or to shorten the length to keep the dog near you.

COLLAR

Your pup should get used to wearing a collar all the time since you will want to attach his ID tags to it; plus, you have to attach the lead to something! A lightweight nylon collar is a good choice. Make certain that the collar fits snugly enough so that the pup cannot wriggle out of it, but is loose enough so that it will not be uncomfortably tight around the pup's neck. Keep in mind that the collar must fit not only around the dog's neck but also around the fluffy coat. You should be able to fit a finger between the pup's neck and the collar. It may take some time for your pup to get used to wearing the collar, but soon he will not even notice that it is there.

Choke collars are made for training, but are in no way suitable for use on the Coton, as they should never be used on small dogs and coated breeds.

MENTAL AND DENTAL
Toys not only help your puppy get the physical and mental stimulation he needs but also provide a great way to keep his teeth clean. Hard rubber or nylon toys, especially those constructed with grooves, are designed to scrape away plaque, preventing bad breath and gum infection.

CHOOSE AN APPROPRIATE COLLAR

The **BUCKLE COLLAR** is the standard collar used for everyday purposes. Be sure that you adjust the buckle on growing puppies. Check it every day. It can become too tight overnight! These collars can be made of leather or nylon. Attach your dog's identification tags to this collar.

The **CHOKE COLLAR** is designed for training. It is constructed of highly polished steel so that it slides easily through the stainless steel loop. The idea is that the dog controls the pressure around his neck and he will stop pulling if the collar becomes uncomfortable. *Never* use a choke collar on your Coton de Tuléar.

The **HALTER** is for a trained dog that has to be restrained to prevent running away, chasing a cat and the like. Considered the most humane of all collars, it is frequently used on smaller dogs on which collars are not comfortable.

Your local pet shop sells an array of dishes and bowls for water and food.

PHOTO COURTESY OF MIKKI PET PRODUCTS.

FOOD AND WATER BOWLS

Your pup will need two bowls, one for food and one for water. You may want two sets of bowls, one for indoors and one for outdoors, depending on where the dog will be fed and where he will be spending time. Stainless steel or sturdy plastic bowls are popular choices. Plastic bowls are more chewable, but dogs tend not to chew on the steel variety, which can be sterilized. It is important to buy sturdy bowls since anything is in danger of being chewed by puppy teeth and you do not want your dog to be constantly chewing apart his bowl (for his safety and for your purse!).

CLEANING SUPPLIES

Until your pup is house-trained, you will be doing a lot of cleaning. Accidents will occur, which is acceptable in the beginning stages of toilet training because the puppy does not know any better. All you can do is be prepared to clean up any accidents as soon as they happen. Old bath towels, paper towels, newspapers and a safe disinfectant are good to have on hand.

BEYOND THE BASICS

The items previously discussed are the bare necessities. You will find out what else you need as you go along—grooming supplies, flea/tick protection, baby gates to partition a room, etc. These things will vary depending on your situation, but it is important that you have everything you need to feed and make your Coton de Tuléar comfortable in his first few days at home.

PUPPY-PROOFING YOUR HOME

Aside from making sure that your Coton will be comfortable in your home, you also have to make sure that your home is safe for your Coton. This means taking precautions that your pup will not get into anything he should not get into and that there is nothing within his reach that may harm him should he sniff it, chew it, inspect it, etc. This probably seems obvious since, while you are primarily concerned with your pup's safety, at the same time you do not want your belongings to be ruined. Breakables should be placed out of reach if your dog is to have full run of the house. If he is to be limited to certain places within the house, keep any potentially dangerous items in the "off-limits" areas.

An electrical cord can pose a danger should the puppy decide to taste it—and who is going to convince a pup that it would not make a great chew toy? All cords and wires should be fastened tightly against the wall,

out of puppy's sight and away from his teeth. If your dog is going to spend time in a crate, make sure that there is nothing near his crate that he can reach

PLAY'S THE THING
Teaching your Coton to play with his toys in running and fetching games is an ideal way to help him develop muscle, learn motor skills and bond with you, his owner and master. He also needs to learn how to inhibit his bite reflex and never to use his teeth on people, forbidden objects and other animals in play. Whenever you play with your Coton, you make the rules. This becomes an important message to your dog in teaching him that you are the pack leader and control everything he does in life. Once your dog accepts you as his leader, your relationship with him will be cemented for life.

NATURAL TOXINS

Examine your grass and landscaping before bringing your puppy home. Many varieties of plants have leaves, stems or flowers that are toxic if ingested, and you can depend on a curious puppy to investigate them. Ask your vet for information on poisonous plants or research them at your library.

If you see your dog carrying a piece of vegetation in his mouth, approach him in a quiet, disinterested manner, avoid eye contact, pet him and gradually remove the plant from his mouth. Alternatively, offer him a treat and maybe he'll drop the plant on his own accord. Be sure no toxic plants are growing in your own yard or kept in your home.

if he sticks his curious little nose or paws through the openings. Just as you would with a child, keep all household cleaners and chemicals where the pup cannot reach them.

It is also important to make sure that the outside of your home is safe. Of course, your puppy should never be unsupervised, but a pup let loose in the yard will want to run and explore, and he should be granted that freedom. Do not let a fence give you a false sense of security; you would be surprised at how crafty (and persistent) a dog can be in working out how to dig under and squeeze his way through small holes, or to jump or climb over a fence. With the Coton's being a very skilled climber, it is not really difficult for him to scale even high fences. Although it is not necessary for you to turn your yard into another Fort Knox, a fence of at least 2 meters (6–7 feet) in height can save you a lot of worries. The fence should also be well embedded into the ground to prevent the dog from digging underneath.

Check the fence periodically to ensure that it is in good shape and make repairs as needed. A very determined pup may return to the same spot to "work on it" until he is able to get through.

FIRST TRIP TO THE VET

You have selected your puppy, and your home and family are ready. Now all you have to do is collect your Coton from the breeder and the fun begins, right? Well...not so fast. Something else you need to plan is your pup's first trip to the vet. Perhaps the breeder can recommend someone in your area, or maybe you know some other dog owners who can suggest a good vet. If you can find a vet who has experience with the Coton, all the better! Either way, you should have an appointment arranged for your pup before you pick him up.

The pup's first visit will consist of an overall examination to make sure that he does not have any problems that are not apparent to you. The vet will also set up a schedule for the pup's vaccinations; the breeder will inform you of

which ones the pup has already received and the vet can continue from there.

INTRODUCTION TO THE FAMILY

Everyone in the house will be excited about the puppy's coming home and will want to pet him and play with him, but it is best to make the introduction low-key so as not to overwhelm the puppy. He is apprehensive already. It is the first time he has been separated from

CHEMICAL TOXINS

Scour your garage for potential doggie dangers. Remove weed killers, pesticides and antifreeze materials. Antifreeze is highly toxic and just a few drops can kill a puppy or an adult dog. The sweet taste attracts the animal, who will quickly consume it from the floor or pavement.

Is there any doubt that you will own the first Coton de Tuléar in your neighborhood? Take your prized pet out to socialize with your friends and neighbors. Socialization and lead training go hand in hand.

his mother and the breeder, and the ride to your home is likely to be the first time he has been in a car. The last thing you want to do is smother him, as this will only frighten him further. This is not to say that human contact is not extremely necessary at this stage, because this is the time when a connection between the pup and his human family is formed. Gentle petting and soothing words should help console him, as well as just putting him down and letting him explore on his own (under your watchful eye, of course).

The pup may approach the family members or may busy himself with exploring for a while. Gradually, each person should spend some time with the pup, one at a time, crouching down to get as close to the pup's level as possible, letting him sniff each person's hands and petting him gently. He definitely needs human attention and he needs to be touched— this is how to form an immediate bond. Just remember that the pup is experiencing many things for the first time, at the same time. There are new people, new noises, new smells and new things to investigate, so be gentle, be affectionate and be as comforting as you can be.

HOW VACCINES WORK

Experienced breeders administer their own vaccines and explain to you the importance of having your pup vaccinated, but do you understand how vaccines work? Vaccines contain the same bacteria or viruses that cause the disease you want to prevent, but they have been chemically modified so that they don't cause any harm. Instead, the vaccine causes your dog to produce antibodies that fight the harmful bacteria. Thus, if your dog is exposed to the disease in the future, the antibodies will destroy the viruses or bacteria.

PUP'S FIRST NIGHT HOME

You have traveled home with your new charge safely in his crate. He's been to the vet for a thorough checkup; he's been weighed, his papers have been examined and perhaps he's even been vaccinated and wormed as well. He's met (and licked!) the whole family, including the excited children and the less-

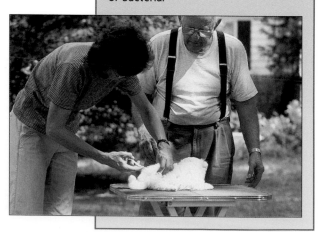

than-happy cat. He's explored his area, his new bed, the yard and anywhere else he's been permitted. He's eaten his first meal at home and relieved himself in the proper place. He's heard lots of new sounds, smelled new friends and seen more of the outside world than ever before...and that was just the first day! He's worn out and is ready for bed...or so you think!

It's puppy's first night home and you are ready to say "Good night." Keep in mind that this is his first night ever to be sleeping alone. His dam and littermates are no longer at paw's length and he's a bit scared, cold and lonely. Be reassuring to your new family member, but this is not the time to spoil him and give in to his inevitable crying/whining.

A puppy Coton may prefer to chew on your old shoes—though nylon bones and dog toys are more affordable.

Puppies whine. They whine to let others know where they are and hopefully to get company out of it. Place your pup in his new bed or crate in his designated area and close the crate door. Mercifully, he may fall asleep without a peep. When the inevitable occurs, however, ignore the whining— he is fine. Be strong and keep his interest in mind. Do not allow yourself to feel guilty and visit the pup. He will fall asleep eventually.

Many breeders recommend placing a piece of bedding from the pup's former home in his new bed so that he recognizes and is comforted by the scent of his littermates. Others still advise placing a hot water bottle

THE COCOA WARS

Chocolate contains the chemical thebromine, which is poisonous to dogs, although "chocolates" especially made for dogs are safe (as they don't actually contain chocolate) but not recommended. Any item that encourages your dog to enjoy the taste of cocoa should be discouraged. You should also exercise caution when using mulch in your garden. This frequently contains cocoa hulls, and dogs have been known to die from eating mulch.

in the bed for warmth. The latter may be a good idea provided the pup doesn't attempt to suckle—he'll get good and wet, and may not fall asleep so fast.

Puppy's first night can be somewhat stressful for both the pup and his new family. Remember that you are setting the tone of nighttime at your house. Unless you want to play with your pup every night at 10 p.m., midnight and 2 a.m., don't initiate the habit. Your family will thank you, and eventually so will your pup!

PREVENTING PUPPY PROBLEMS

SOCIALIZATION

Now that you have done all of the preparatory work and have helped your pup get accustomed to his new home and family, it is about time for you to have

> Nothing pleases your dog as much as praise! Encourage the Coton for correct behavior and that's all you will ever have from your dog.

> **PUPPY PROBLEMS**
> The majority of problems that are commonly seen in young pups will disappear as your dog gets older. However, how you deal with problems when he is young will determine how he reacts to discipline as an adult dog. It is important to establish who is boss (hopefully it will be you!) right away when you are first bonding with your dog. This bond will set the tone for the rest of your life together.

some fun! Socializing your Coton pup gives you the opportunity to show off your new friend; likely your neighbors have never met this enchanting rare breed. Your pup gets to reap the benefits of being an adorable fluffy creature that people will want to pet and, in general, think is absolutely precious!

Besides getting to know his new family, your puppy should be exposed to other people, animals and situations. This will help him become well adjusted as he grows up and less prone to being timid or fearful of the new things he will encounter. Of course, he must not come into close contact with dogs you don't know well until his course of injections is fully complete.

Your pup's socialization began with the breeder, but now it is your responsibility to continue it. The socialization he receives in the first few weeks after coming home is the most critical, as this is the time when he forms his impressions of the outside world. The eight-to-ten-week-old period is also known as the fear period; during this time, the breeder ensures that the puppy receives gentle and reassuring interaction. Lack of socialization, and/or negative experiences during the socialization period, can manifest itself in fear and aggression as the dog grows up. Your puppy needs lots of positive interaction, which of course includes human contact, affection, handling and exposure to other animals. Luckily, your Coton is a gregarious little creature that can't wait to meet new friends!

Once your pup has received his necessary vaccinations, feel

No matter how talented the Coton breed is, no dog can train himself. You as the owner must invest time and energy in your Coton's education and repertoire of basic commands.

free to take him out and about (on his lead, of course). Walk him around the neighborhood, take him on your daily errands, let people pet him, let him meet other dogs and pets, etc. Puppies do not have to try to make friends; there will be no shortage of people who will want to introduce themselves. Just make sure that you carefully supervise each meeting. If the neighborhood children want to say hello, for example, that is great—children and pups most often make great companions. However, sometimes an excited child can unintentionally handle a pup too roughly, or an overzealous pup can playfully nip a little too hard. You want to make socialization experi-

PUP MEETS WORLD

Thorough socialization includes not only meeting new people but also being introduced to new experiences such as riding in the car, having his coat brushed, hearing the television, walking in a crowd—the list is endless. The more your pup experiences, and the more positive the experiences are, the less of a shock and the less frightening it will be for your pup to encounter new things.

ences positive ones. What a pup learns during this very formative stage will affect his attitude toward future encounters. You want your dog to be comfortable around everyone. A pup that has a bad experience with a child may grow up to be a dog that is shy around or aggressive toward children.

CONSISTENCY IN TRAINING

Dogs, being pack animals, naturally need a leader, or else they try to establish dominance in their packs. When you welcome a dog into your family, the choice of who becomes the leader and who becomes the pack is entirely up to you! Your pup's intuitive quest for dominance, coupled with the fact that it is nearly impossible to say "No" to a Coton when he peers out from under his cottony tufts with twinkling eyes, give the pup an almost unfair advantage in getting the upper hand!

A pup will definitely test the waters to see what he can and cannot do. Do not give in to those pleading eyes—stand your ground when it comes to disciplining the pup and make sure that all family members do the same. It will only confuse the pup if Mother tells him to get off the sofa when he is used to sitting up there with Father to watch the nightly news. Avoid discrepancies by having all members of the household decide on the rules before the pup even comes home...and be consistent in enforcing them! Early training shapes the dog's personality, so you cannot be unclear in what you expect.

MANNERS MATTER

During the socialization process, a puppy should meet people, experience different environments and definitely be exposed to other canines. Through playing and interacting with other dogs, your Coton will learn lessons, ranging from controlling the pressure of his jaws by biting his littermates to the inner-workings of the canine pack that he will apply to his human relationships for the rest of his life. That is why removing a puppy from the litter too early can be detrimental to the pup's development.

CHEWING TIPS

Chewing goes hand in hand with nipping in the sense that a teething puppy is always looking for a way to soothe his aching gums. In this case, instead of chewing on you, he may have taken a liking to your favorite shoe or something else that he should not be chewing. Again, realize that this is a normal canine behavior that does not need to be discouraged, only redirected. Your pup just needs to be taught what is acceptable to chew on and what is off-limits. Consistently tell him "No!" when you catch him chewing on something forbidden and give him a chew toy.

Conversely, praise him when you catch him chewing on something appropriate. In this way, you are discouraging the inappropriate behavior and reinforcing the desired behavior. The puppy's chewing should stop after his adult teeth have come in, but an adult dog continues to chew for various reasons—perhaps because he is bored, needs to relieve tension or just likes to chew. That is why it is important to redirect his chewing when he is still young.

COMMON PUPPY PROBLEMS

The best way to prevent puppy problems is to be proactive in stopping an undesirable behavior as soon as it starts. The old saying "You can't teach an old dog new tricks" does not necessarily hold true, but it *is* true that it is much easier to discourage bad behavior in a young developing pup than to wait until the pup's bad behavior becomes the adult dog's bad habit. There are some problems that are especially prevalent in puppies as they develop.

NIPPING

As puppies start to teethe, they feel the need to sink their teeth into anything available...unfortunately, that usually includes your fingers, arms, hair and toes. You may find this behavior cute for about the first five seconds...until you feel just how sharp those puppy teeth are. Nipping is something you want to discourage immediately and consistently with a firm "No!" (or whatever number of firm "Nos" it takes for him to understand that you mean business). Then, replace your finger with an appropriate chew toy. While this behavior is merely annoying when the dog is young, it can become dangerous as your Coton's adult teeth grow in and his jaws develop, and he continues to think it is okay to gnaw on human appendages. Your Coton does not mean any harm with a friendly nip, but he also does not know that his nipping doesn't feel so friendly!

CRYING/WHINING

Your pup will often cry, whine, whimper, howl or make some type of commotion when he is left alone. This is basically his way of calling out for attention to make sure that you know he is there and that you have not forgotten about him. Your puppy feels insecure when he is left alone, when you are out of the house and he is in his crate or when you are in another part of the house and he cannot see you. The noise he is making is an expression of the anxiety he feels at being alone, so he needs to be taught that being alone is okay. You are not actually training the dog to stop making noise; rather, you are training him to feel comfortable when he is alone and thus removing the need for him to make the noise.

This is where the crate with cozy bedding and a toy comes in handy. You want to know that your pup is safe when you are not there to supervise, and you know that he will be safe in his crate rather than roaming freely about the house. In order for the pup to stay in his crate without making a fuss, he first needs to be comfortable in his crate. On that note, it is extremely important that the crate is never used as a form of punishment; this will cause the pup to view the crate as a negative place, rather than as a place of his own for safety and retreat.

Accustom the pup to the crate in short, gradually increasing time intervals in which you put him in the crate, maybe with a treat, and stay in the room with him. If he cries or makes a fuss, do not go to him, but stay in his sight. Gradually he will realize that staying in his crate is just fine without your help, and it will not be so traumatic for him when you are not around. You may want to leave the radio on softly when you leave the house; the sound of human voices may be comforting to him.

> **LEARNING BY CHEWING**
> Pups learn a great deal about their environment from taking everything into their mouths. A puppy will investigate anything and everything he can get his teeth on. You, as an owner, must ensure that all potentially dangerous items (power cables, chemicals, breakables, etc.) are beyond the pup's reach or kept in areas that are off-limits to him. Once the pup has gained enough confidence, he will explore wherever in the house he is allowed to go, so take this into consideration when setting boundaries and creating a safe environment for the pup.

DIETARY AND FEEDING CONSIDERATIONS

Today the choices of food for your Coton de Tuléar are many and varied. There are simply dozens of brands of food in all sorts of flavors and textures, ranging from puppy diets to those for seniors. There are even hypoallergenic and low-calorie diets available. Because your Coton's food has a bearing on coat, health and temperament, it is essential that the most suitable diet is selected for a dog of his age. It is fair to say, however, that even experienced owners can be perplexed by the enormous range of foods available. Only understanding what is best for your dog will help you reach an informed decision.

Dog foods are produced in three basic types: dry, semi-moist and canned. Dry foods are useful for the cost-conscious, for overall they tend to be less expensive than semi-moist or canned foods. Dry foods also contain the least fat and the most preservatives. In general, canned foods are made up of 60–70% water, while semi-moist ones often contain so much sugar that they are perhaps the least preferred by owners, even though their dogs seem to like them.

When selecting your dog's diet, three stages of development

GRAIN-BASED DIETS

Some less expensive dog foods are based on grains and other plant proteins. While these products may appear to be attractively priced, many breeders prefer a diet based on animal proteins and believe that they are more conducive to your dog's health. Many grain-based diets rely on soy protein, which may cause flatulence (passing gas).

There are many cases, however, when your dog might require a special diet. These special requirements should only be recommended by your veterinarian.

must be considered: the puppy stage, the adult stage and the senior stage.

PUPPY STAGE

Puppies instinctively want to suck milk from their mother's teats; a normal puppy will exhibit this behavior just a few moments following birth. If puppies do not attempt to suckle within the first half-hour or so, the breeder should encourage them to do so by placing them on the nipples, having selected ones with plenty of milk. This early milk supply is important in providing the essential colostrum, which protects the puppies during the first eight to ten weeks of their lives. Although a mother's milk is much better than any commercially prepared milk formula, despite there being some excellent ones available, if the puppies do not feed, the breeder will have to feed them by hand. For those with less experience, advice from a vet is important so that not only the right quantity of milk is fed but also that of correct quality, fed at suitably frequent intervals, usually every two hours during the first few days of life.

Puppies should be allowed to nurse from their dam for about the first six weeks, although, starting around the third or fourth week, the breeder will begin to introduce small portions of suitable solid food. Most breeders like to introduce alternate milk and meat meals initially, building up to weaning time.

By the time the puppies are seven or a maximum of eight

Mother's milk is best for the Coton during the first weeks of his life. Some Coton litters can be as small as one pup!

weeks old, they should be fully weaned and fed solely on a proprietary puppy food. Your breeder should provide you with a diet sheet when you bring your puppy home so that you know the type of food he has been getting, and how much and when he has been eating. You should continue on a similar schedule with the same food if possible. Feeding the most suitable, good-quality diet at this time is essential, for a puppy's fastest growth rate is during the first year of life.

As your puppy grows, the frequency of meals will be reduced, and eventually you will switch to an adult dog food. Your vet and breeder are good sources of advice about the optimal age to switch and a good adult-maintenance diet. Commercially prepared puppy and junior diets, as well as adult diets, should be well balanced for the needs of your dog so that, except in certain circumstances, additional vitamins, minerals and proteins will not be required.

ADULT DIETS

A dog is considered an adult when he has stopped growing, although a dog can reach full size before reaching full physical maturity. Take your breeder's advice about switching your Coton to an adult diet. The breeder will be familiar with how his bloodline develops and will

FOOD PREFERENCE

Selecting the best dog food is difficult. There is no majority consensus among veterinary scientists as to the value of nutrient analysis (protein, fat, fiber, moisture, ash, cholesterol, minerals, etc.). All agree that feeding trials are what matter most, but you also have to consider the individual dog. The dog's weight, age and activity level, and what pleases his taste, all must be considered. It is best to take the advice of your veterinarian. Every dog's dietary requirements vary, even during the lifetime of a particular dog.

If your dog is fed a good dry food, he does not require supplements of meat or vegetables. Dogs do appreciate a little variety in their diets, so you may choose to stay with the same brand but vary the flavor. Alternatively, you may wish to add a little flavored stock to give a difference to the taste.

be able to suggest the proper age at which to make the switch, as well as a suitable food and amounts to feed.

Major dog-food manufacturers specialize in adult-maintenance food, and it is merely necessary for you to select the one best suited to your Coton's needs. Active dogs may have different requirements from more sedate dogs. Again, commercial foods should be nutritionally balanced; if supplementation of any kind becomes necessary, it should only be given as prescribed by the vet.

SENIOR DIETS

As dogs get older, their metabolism changes. The older dog usually exercises less, moves more slowly and sleeps more. This change in lifestyle and physiological performance requires a change in diet. Since these changes take place slowly, they might not be recognizable. What is easily recognizable is weight gain. By continuing to feed your

CHANGE IN DIET

As your dog's caretaker, you know the importance of keeping his diet consistent, but sometimes when you run out of food or if you're on vacation, you have to make a change quickly. Some dogs will experience digestive problems, but most will not. If you are planning on changing your dog's menu, do so gradually to ensure that your dog will not have any problems. Over a period of four to five days, slowly add some new food to your dog's old food, increasing the percentage of new food each day.

dog an adult-maintenance diet when he is slowing down metabolically, your dog will gain weight. Obesity in an older dog compounds the health problems that already accompany old age and can cause problems on its own as well.

As your dog gets older, few of his organs function up to par. The kidneys slow down and the intestines become less efficient. These age-related factors are best handled with a change in diet and a change in feeding schedule to give smaller portions that are more easily digested. There is no single best diet for every dog. While many dogs do well on light or senior diets, other dogs do better on puppy diets or other special premium diets such as lamb and rice. Be sensitive to your senior Coton's diet, as this

Puppies are introduced to solid food as part of the weaning process.

will help control other problems that may arise with your old friend.

WATER

Just as your dog needs proper nutrition from his food, water is an essential "nutrient" as well. Water keeps the dog's body properly hydrated and promotes normal function of the body's systems. During house-training, it is necessary to keep an eye on how much water your Coton is drinking, but once he is reliably trained he should have access to clean fresh water at all times, especially if you feed dry food. Make certain that the dog's water bowl is clean, and change the water often.

EXERCISE

All dogs require some form of exercise, regardless of breed. A sedentary lifestyle is as harmful to a dog as it is to a person. The Coton is a fairly active breed that enjoys and will appreciate exercise, but you don't have to be an Olympic athlete to provide your dog with a sufficient amount of activity! Exercising your Coton can be enjoyable and healthy for both of you. Brisk walks, once the puppy reaches three or four months of age, will stimulate heart rates and build muscle for both dog and owner. As the dog reaches adulthood, the speed and distance of the walks can be

DRINK, DRANK, DRUNK—MAKE IT A DOUBLE

In both humans and dogs, as well as other living organisms, water forms the major part of nearly every body tissue. Naturally, we take water for granted, but without it, life as we know it would cease.

For dogs, water is needed to keep their bodies functioning biochemically. Additionally, water is needed to replace the water lost while panting. Unlike humans, who are able to sweat to dissipate heat, dogs must pant to cool down, thereby losing the vital water that their bodies need to regulate their body temperatures. Humans lose electrolyte-containing products and other body-fluid components through sweating; dogs do not lose anything except water.

Water is essential always, but especially so when the weather is hot or humid or when your dog is exercising or working vigorously.

increased as long as they are both kept reasonable and comfortable for both of you.

Play sessions in the fenced yard and letting the dog run free in your yard or another fenced enclosure under your supervision also are sufficient forms of exercise for the Coton. Fetching games can be played indoors or out; these are excellent for giving your dog active play that he will enjoy. With a small dog like the Coton, games can easily be played indoors to give him the exercise he needs no matter the weather. Going after things that move comes naturally to dogs of all breeds, and the Coton has a bit of the terrier "fire" in him when it comes to the chase.

When your Coton runs after the ball or object, praise him for picking it up and encourage him to bring it back to you for another throw. Never go to the object and pick it up yourself, or you'll soon find that you are the one retriev-

A fussy Coton is created only by spoiling. Young pups compete around the food and water bowls. Healthy pups want a healthy share!

> **TIPPING THE SCALES**
> Good nutrition is vital to your dog's health, but many people end up over-feeding or giving unnecessary supplements. Here are some common doggie diet don'ts:
> • Adding milk, yogurt and cheese to your dog's diet may seem like a good idea for coat and skin care, but dairy products are very fattening and can cause indigestion.
> • Diets high in fat will not cause heart attacks in dogs but will certainly cause your dog to gain weight.
> • Most importantly, don't assume your dog will simply stop eating once he doesn't need any more food. Given the chance, he will eat you out of house and home!

ing the objects rather than the dog! If you choose to play games outdoors, you must have a securely fenced-in yard and/or have the dog attached to at least a 25-foot (about 8-meter) light line for security. You want your Coton to run, but not run away!

Bear in mind that an overweight dog should never be suddenly over-exercised; instead, he should be encouraged to increase exercise slowly. Remember that exercise is not only essential to keep the dog's body fit, but it is also essential to his mental well-being. A bored dog will find something to do, which often manifests itself in

some type of destructive behavior. In this sense, exercise is just as essential for the owner's mental well-being!

GROOMING

ROUTINE MAINTENANCE

The most prominent physical feature of this breed is its beautiful coat, which consists of long, white, heavy hair. It is fluffy in texture rather than silky. Maintaining the coat's cotton-like texture means taking care of it on a regular basis. The hair of your Coton should be combed and brushed at least twice a week. Neglecting basic grooming duties results in the formation of tangles and mats, which will spoil the

GROOMING NEEDS

Invest in quality grooming tools that will withstand frequent use. Here are some basics:

- Slicker brush
- Bristle brush
- Metal comb
- Scissors
- Rubber mat
- Dog shampoo
- Spray hose attachment
- Blow dryer
- Towels
- Ear cleaner
- Cotton balls
- Nail clippers
- Dental care products
- Tear-stain remover

coat. Also to avoid matting and potential skin irritations, you must check the coat carefully after any time spent outdoors and remove all burrs, dry grass, thorns and whatever else may have become attached to the coat. Despite the breed's very unique coat, you do not need specialized equipment for grooming the Coton; suitable grooming tools can be found in every pet shop.

An old proverb says, "Fine feathers make fine birds." Applying this to our Coton de Tuléar, it means that a well-

Champion Cotons have knock-out coats that are groomed to their natural perfection. This Coton certainly has some mighty fine feathers!

Accustom your Coton puppy to the brushing regimen as soon as your bring him home. In no time, your Coton will look forward to this special time together.

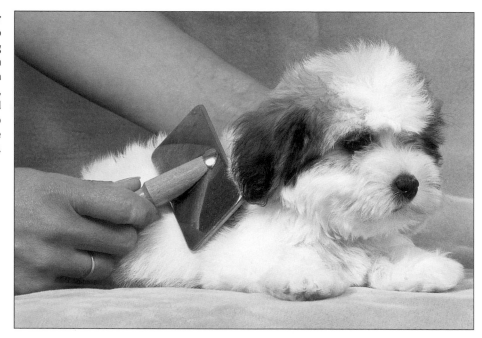

(Left) Brushing your Coton daily will make the coat look its best and stimulate the coat's natural oils to keep the skin healthy, too. A slicker brush is useful on the adult and puppy alike. (Right) Purchase a grooming table that can be adjusted to a comfortable height for you.

The grooming table is useful for more than just your Coton's beauty sessions. Future show dogs can be trained to stand on the table so they are accustomed to doing so when it comes time for a turn in front of a show judge.

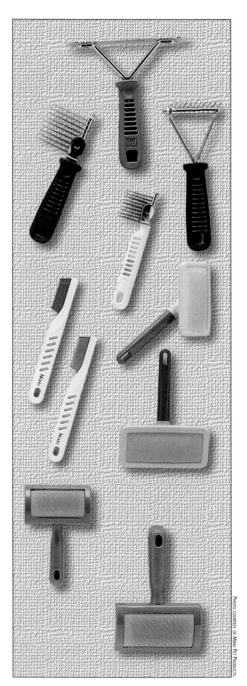

PHOTO COURTESY OF MIKKI PET PRODUCTS

groomed Coton is beautiful. Carefully kept in prime condition with comb and brush, your Coton de Tuléar will be a feast for the eyes at all times.

BATHING

Dog owners are passionate in their arguments about the appropriate frequency of baths. You should therefore trust your own instincts and bathe your Coton only when it is really necessary. An old rule of thumb says, "As rarely as possible, but as often as necessary." Although this leaves a lot of room for interpretation, it is actually makes a succinct point when you think about it. Every six months is surely a bit too long in between baths, but weekly baths are certainly far too frequent. Under normal circumstances, a bath every six to eight weeks should be sufficient.

Despite the Coton's white coat, it is neither necessary nor beneficial to expose the dog's skin and hair too often to bathing, as essential oils and proteins are lost during bathing. When bathing does become necessary, you should only use a shampoo specifically formulated for long-haired, white dogs. Even after an extensive walk in the rain or snow, the dog does not necessarily need to be bathed. It may be entirely sufficient just to rub him dry, as most of the dirt will fall out of the coat when the coat dries, and what remains can be removed with a thorough brushing.

When you do bathe your Coton, brush him thoroughly before wetting his coat to get rid of most mats and tangles, which are harder to remove when the coat is wet. Make certain that your dog has a good non-slip surface on which to stand. Begin by wetting the dog's coat, checking the water temperature to make sure that it is neither too hot nor too cold. A shower or hose attachment is necessary for thoroughly wetting and rinsing the coat.

Next, apply shampoo to the dog's coat and work it into a good lather. Wash the head last, as you do not want shampoo to drip into the dog's eyes while you are washing the rest of his body. Work the shampoo all the way down to the skin. You can use this opportunity to check the skin for any bumps, bites or other abnormalities. Do not neglect any area of the body—get all of the hard-to-reach places.

Once the dog has been thoroughly shampooed, he requires an equally thorough rinsing. Shampoo left in the coat can be irritating to the dog's skin. Protect his eyes from the shampoo by shielding them with your hand and directing the flow of water in the opposite direction. You also should avoid getting water in the ear canal. Be prepared for your dog to shake out his coat—you

NAIL CARE
You can purchase nail clippers made for dogs or an electric tool to grind down your dog's nails rather than cut them. Some dogs don't seem to mind the electric grinder but will object strongly to nail clippers. A nail file made for dogs is another option; this is a good choice for the black-nailed Coton de Tuléar.

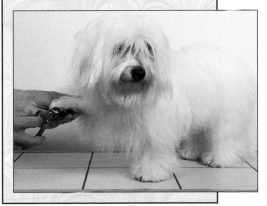

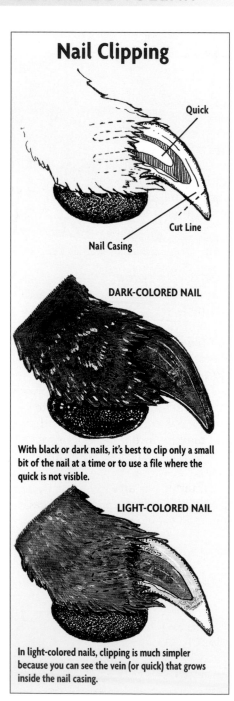

Nail Clipping

Quick

Cut Line

Nail Casing

DARK-COLORED NAIL

With black or dark nails, it's best to clip only a small bit of the nail at a time or to use a file where the quick is not visible.

LIGHT-COLORED NAIL

In light-colored nails, clipping is much simpler because you can see the vein (or quick) that grows inside the nail casing.

might want to stand back, but make sure you have a towel ready and a hold on the dog to keep him from running through the house.

FEET AND NAILS
Grooming also includes the feet and nails. In order to prevent knots of hair from forming between the pads of the feet, the hair should be trimmed with a round-tipped pair of scissors. For a well-groomed appearance, the hair around the nails should also be trimmed.

Small dogs are lightweight and, for this simple reason, do not wear down their nails sufficiently; therefore, the nails have to be cut back from time to time. A good tool for this task is a nail clipper for dogs, as it is easy to use. A disadvantage of clipping the nails is, however, that it triggers the "quick" (the blood vessel that runs through each nail) to grow forward. This can be avoided by filing the nails down rather than clipping them.

The nails of the show-quality Coton are black, making it difficult to see the quick, so you must take care in finding the proper length without nipping the quick. The quick will bleed if accidentally cut, which will be quite painful for the dog as it contains nerve endings. Keep some type of clotting agent on hand, such as a styptic pencil or styptic powder (the type used for shaving). This will stop the bleeding quickly when applied to the end of the cut nail. Do not panic if you cut the quick, just stop the bleeding and talk soothingly to your dog. Once he has calmed down, move on to the next nail. It is better to clip or file only a little at a time.

Hold your pup steady as you begin trimming his nails; you do not want him to make any sudden movements or run away. Talk to him soothingly and stroke him as you clip or file, holding his foot in your hand.

Ear Cleaning

With ears that hang down, it is of great importance that they are looked after properly. Ear-mite infestations are common, so regular checks of the ears are necessary. If your Coton has been shaking his head or scratching at his ears frequently, this usually indicates a problem. If the dog's ears have an unusual odor, this is a sure sign of mite infestation or infection, and a signal to have his ears checked by the vet.

A good preventative measure is to pluck the hairs growing inside the ears as part of your grooming routine. This enables unobstructed discharge of ear wax and proper ventilation inside the ear. The ears can be kept clean with a soft cotton ball or wipe, and an ear powder or liquid made especially for dogs. Never probe into the ear canal, as this can cause injury.

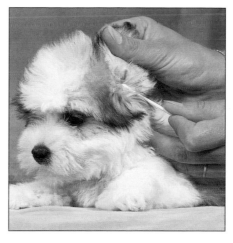

Be very careful and gentle when cleaning your Coton's ears. Use a soft piece of cotton with powder or liquid ear cleaner. Never probe into the ear canal.

Care of the Teeth

The maintenance of a healthy and complete set of teeth is important for your Coton. It is an unfortunate fact that gum disease is particularly common among small dog breeds, causing an early loss of teeth despite regular care. Some bloodlines appear to be more prone to problems in this regard than others and may require more intensive care to maintain their teeth for as long as possible.

If tartar has already formed, a thorough cleaning, including scaling, is in order. This should only

DEADLY DECAY

Did you know that periodontal disease (a condition of the bone and gums surrounding a tooth) can be fatal? Having your dog's teeth and mouth checked yearly can prevent it.

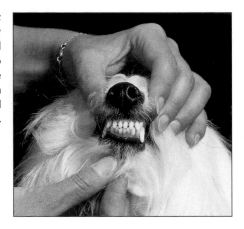

The Coton's coat isn't the only thing that should be white! Keep your Coton's smile gleaming through proper care and attention.

be done by a vet, as unprofessional treatment may result in an inflammation of the gums.

In order to prevent tartar from forming in the first place, it is advisable to brush your Coton's teeth with a toothbrush and tooth-

Yes, we brush our dogs' teeth, too! Tooth-brushing keeps the teeth clean, the gums healthy and the breath fresh.

paste, both made for dogs, once a week. If your Coton is accustomed to the procedure in puppyhood, he will tolerate it without resistance as an adult.

TEAR STAINS
The tear glands of the eyes discharge fluid on a continuous basis. The fluid normally runs off via a canal into the nasal cavity. Some dogs may suffer from a blockage of this canal or constricted ducts due to a birth defect, resulting in an overflow of tears. The tear fluid then spills over onto the face, staining the facial hair beneath the eyes; in extreme cases, these tear stains can be an unsightly color of dark brown.

In order to prevent tear stains, the region below the eyes should be kept clean and dry. You should use a tear-stain remover for this purpose, available from vets and well-stocked pet shops. It is applied with a lint-free piece of cloth from the outer to the inner corner of the area under the eye. In the case of a dog suffering badly from tear staining, cleaning should be done several times a day.

ANAL GLANDS
Perhaps the least pleasant task in your grooming routine is the emptying of the anal glands. In most dogs, the glands express themselves, resulting in a

discharge of a foul-smelling secretion; this is normal. In other dogs, the glands do not express themselves, which can lead to a problem. Many dog owners will notice that their dogs rub their behinds vigorously on the ground, obviously in an attempt to relieve a serious itch. This could point to blocked anal glands.

The glands are situated to the left and right of the anus and should empty themselves during defecation. If the natural discharge is hindered, the glands have to be expressed manually. This is done by squeezing the glands between two of your fingers, pushing in an upward manner, so that the accumulated fluid can flow out. The liquid is then caught with a piece of absorbent cloth or a sponge. In more severe cases, a veterinarian may need to perform the expression of the dog's anal glands.

TRAVELING WITH YOUR DOG

CAR TRAVEL

You should accustom your Coton to riding in a car at an early age. You may or may not take him in the car often, but at the very least he will need to go to the vet and you do not want these trips to be traumatic for the dog or troublesome for you. The safest way for a dog to ride in the car is in his crate. If he uses a crate in the house, you can use the same crate for travel.

Put the pup in the crate and see how he reacts. If he seems uneasy, you can have a passenger hold him on his lap while you drive. Another option for car travel is a specially made safety harness for dogs, which straps the dog in much like a seat belt. Do not let the dog roam loose in the vehicle—this is very dangerous! If you should stop short, your dog

Consider having your Coton tattooed for safety. Your vet should be able to advise you in this regard. The belly or inner thigh is the most common place to have a Coton tattooed.

can be thrown and injured. If the dog starts climbing on you and pestering you while you are driving, you will not be able to concentrate on the road. It is an unsafe situation for everyone—human and canine. Equally unsafe is leaving the dog alone in the car—don't do it, not even for a minute!

For long trips, be prepared to stop to let the dog relieve himself. Take with you whatever you need to clean up after him, including some paper towels and some rags for use should he have a potty accident in the car or suffer from motion sickness.

AIR TRAVEL

Contact your chosen airline before proceeding with travel plans that include your Coton. The dog will be required to travel in a fiberglass crate and you should always check in advance with the airline regarding specific requirements for the crate's size, type and labeling, and other regulations. On many airlines, small pets whose crates fall within the specified size limitations are granted "carry-on" status and can accompany their owners in the cabin in their crates. This may be possible with your Coton; again, check with the airline ahead of time.

IDENTIFICATION OPTIONS

As puppies become more and more expensive, especially those puppies of high quality for showing and/or breeding, they have a greater chance of being stolen. The usual collar dog tag is, of course, easily removed. But there are two more permanent techniques that have become widely used for identifying dogs.

The puppy microchip implantation involves the injection of a small microchip, about the size of a corn kernel, under the skin of the dog. If your dog shows up at a clinic or shelter, or is offered for resale under less-than-savory circumstances, he can be positively identified by the microchip. The microchip is scanned, and a registry quickly identifies you as the owner.

Tattooing is done on various parts of the dog, from his belly to his ears. The number tattooed can be your telephone number, the dog's registration number or any other number that you can easily memorize. When professional dog thieves see a tattooed dog, they usually lose interest. For the safety of our dogs, no laboratory facility or dog broker will accept a tattooed dog as stock.

Discuss microchipping and tattooing with your vet and breeder. Some vets perform these services for a reasonable fee. To ensure that the dog's ID is effective, be certain that the dog is then properly registered with a legitimate national database.

Here's a dedicated owner—Cotons to go! Be sure your Coton is secure in his crate before you go for a ride in the car. This is another benefit of crate training your dog.

To help put the dog at ease, give him one of his favorite toys in the crate. Do not feed the dog for several hours prior to checking in for your flight so that you minimize his need to relieve himself. Some airlines require you to provide documentation as to when the dog has last been fed. In any case, a light meal is best.

Make sure your that your Coton is properly identified. If not permitted in the cabin, your Coton will travel in a different area of the plane than the human passengers, so every rule must be strictly followed to prevent any risk of getting separated from your dog.

VACATIONS AND BOARDING

So you want to take a family vacation—and you want to include *all* members of the family. You would probably make arrangements for accommodations ahead of time anyway, but this is especially important when traveling with a dog. You do not want to make an overnight stop at the only place around for miles, only to find out that they do not allow dogs. Also, you do not want to reserve a place for your family without confirming that you are traveling with a dog, because, if it is against the hotel's policy, you may end up without a place to stay.

Alternatively, if you are traveling and choose not to bring your Coton, you will have to make arrangements for him while you are away. Some options are to take him to a neighbor's house to stay while you are gone, to have a trusted neighbor stay at your house or to bring your dog to a reputable boarding kennel. If you choose to board him at a kennel, you should visit in advance to see the facilities provided and where the dogs are kept. Are the dogs' areas spacious and kept clean? Talk to some of the employees and observe how they treat the dogs—do they spend time with the dogs, play with them, exercise them, groom them, etc.? Also find out the kennel's policy on vaccinations and what they require. This is for all of the dogs' safety, since there is a greater risk of diseases being passed from dog to dog when dogs are kept together.

IDENTIFICATION

Your Coton is your valued companion and friend. That is why you always keep a close eye on him and you have made sure that he cannot escape from the yard or wriggle out of his collar and run away from you. However, accidents can happen and there may come a time when your dog unexpectedly becomes separated from you. If this unfortunate event should occur, the first thing on your mind will be finding him. Proper identification will increase the chances of his being returned to you safely and quickly.

A Coton is truly a prized possession. You are responsible for your Coton de Tuléar's safety both in the home and outside. Just as you are liable for your children's safety, so, too, must you be dedicated to your dog's well-being.

TRAINING YOUR

COTON DE TULÉAR

Living with an untrained dog is a lot like owning a piano that you do not know how to play—it is a nice object to look at, but it does not do much more than that to bring you pleasure. Now try taking piano lessons, and suddenly the piano comes alive and brings forth magical sounds and rhythms that set your heart singing and your body swaying.

The same is true with your Coton de Tuléar. Any dog is a big responsibility and, if not trained sensibly, may develop unacceptable behavior that annoys you or could even cause family friction.

To train your Coton, you may like to enroll in an obedience class. Teach your dog good manners as you learn how and why he behaves the way he does. Find out how to communicate with your dog and how to recognize and understand his communications with you. Suddenly the dog takes on a new role in your life—he is clever, interesting, well behaved and fun to be with. He demonstrates his bond of devotion to you daily. In other words, your Coton does wonders for your ego because he constantly reminds

FEAR AGGRESSION

Pups who are subjected to physical abuse during training commonly end up with behavioral problems as adults. One common result of abuse is fear aggression, in which a dog will lash out, bare his teeth, snarl and finally bite someone by whom he feels threatened. For example, your daughter may be playing with the dog one afternoon. As they play hide-and-seek, she backs the dog into a corner and, as she attempts to tease him playfully, he bites her hand. Examine the cause of this behavior. Did your daughter ever hit the dog? Did someone who resembles your daughter hit or scream at the dog?

Fortunately, fear aggression is relatively easy to correct. Have your daughter engage in only positive activities with the dog, such as feeding, petting and walking. She should not give any corrections or negative feedback. If the dog still growls or cowers away from her, allow someone else to accompany them. After approximately one week, the dog should feel that he can rely on her for many positive things, and he will also be prevented from reacting fearfully towards anyone who might resemble her.

The young Coton is like a giant cotton sponge, ready to soak up everything you teach him. Drench him from the beginning and you will have a well-rounded, biddable companion dog by the time he is one year of age and throughout his entire life.

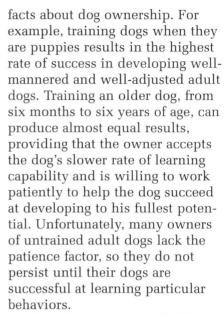

facts about dog ownership. For example, training dogs when they are puppies results in the highest rate of success in developing well-mannered and well-adjusted adult dogs. Training an older dog, from six months to six years of age, can produce almost equal results, providing that the owner accepts the dog's slower rate of learning capability and is willing to work patiently to help the dog succeed at developing to his fullest potential. Unfortunately, many owners of untrained adult dogs lack the patience factor, so they do not persist until their dogs are successful at learning particular behaviors.

Training a puppy aged 10 to 16 weeks (20 weeks at the most) is like working with a dry sponge in a pool of water. The pup soaks up whatever you show him and constantly looks for more things to do and learn. At this early age, his body is not yet producing hormones, and therein lies the reason for such a high rate of success. Without hormones, he is focused on his owners and not particularly interested in investigating other places, dogs, people, etc. You are his leader: his provider of food, water, shelter and security. He latches onto you and wants to stay close. He will usually follow you from room to room, will not let you out of his sight when you are outdoors with him and will respond in like

Communicate with your Coton face to face. Try to understand how your dog thinks and you will succeed more readily in his training.

you that you are not only his leader, you are his hero!

Those involved with teaching dog obedience and counseling owners about their dogs' behavior have discovered some interesting

SAFETY FIRST

While it may seem that the most important things to your dog are eating, sleeping and chewing the upholstery on your furniture, his first concern is actually safety. The domesticated dogs we keep as companions have the same pack instinct as their ancestors who ran free thousands of years ago. Because of this pack instinct, your dog wants to know that he and his pack are not in danger of being harmed, and that his pack has a strong, capable leader. You must establish yourself as the leader early on in your relationship. That way your dog will trust that you will take care of him and the pack, and he will accept your commands without question.

manner to the people and animals you encounter. If you greet a friend warmly, he will be happy to greet the person as well. If, however, you are hesitant or anxious about the approach of a stranger, your puppy will respond accordingly.

Once the puppy begins to produce hormones, his natural curiosity emerges and he begins to investigate the world around him. It is at this time when you may notice that the untrained dog begins to wander away from you and even ignore your commands to stay close. When this behavior becomes a problem, you have two choices: get rid of the dog or train him. It is strongly urged that you choose the latter option.

You usually will be able to find obedience classes within a reasonable distance from your home, but you can also do a lot to train your dog yourself. Sometimes there are classes available, but the tuition is too costly. Whatever the circumstances, the solution to training your Coton de Tuléar without formal obedience classes lies within the pages of this book.

This chapter is devoted to helping you train your Coton at home. If the recommended procedures are followed faithfully, you may expect positive results that will prove rewarding both to you and your dog. Whether your new charge is a puppy or a mature

CALM DOWN
Dogs will do anything for your attention. If you reward the dog when he is calm and attentive, you will develop a well-mannered dog. If, on the other hand, you greet your dog excitedly and encourage him to wrestle with you, the dog will greet you the same way and you will have a hyperactive dog on your hands.

CANINE DEVELOPMENT SCHEDULE

It is important to understand how and at what age a puppy develops into adulthood. If you are a puppy owner, consult the following Canine Development Schedule to determine the stage of development your puppy is currently experiencing. This knowledge will help you as you work with the puppy in the weeks and months ahead.

Period	Age	Characteristics
First to Third	**Birth to Seven Weeks**	Puppy needs food, sleep and warmth, and responds to simple and gentle touching. Needs mother for security and disciplining. Needs littermates for learning and interacting with other dogs. Pup learns to function within a pack and learns pack order of dominance. Begin socializing pup with adults and children for short periods. Pup begins to become aware of his environment.
Fourth	**Eight to Twelve Weeks**	Brain is fully developed. Needs socializing with outside world. Remove from mother and littermates. Needs to change from canine pack to human pack. Human dominance necessary. Fear period occurs between 8 and 12 weeks. Avoid fright and pain.
Fifth	**Thirteen to Sixteen Weeks**	Training and formal obedience should begin. Less association with other dogs, more with people, places, situations. Period will pass easily if you remember this is pup's change-to-adolescence time. Be firm and fair. Flight instinct prominent. Permissiveness and over-disciplining can do permanent damage. Praise for good behavior.
Juvenile	**Four to Eight Months**	Another fear period about 7 to 8 months of age. It passes quickly, but be cautious of fright and pain. Sexual maturity reached around this time. Dominant traits established. Dog should understand sit, down, come and stay by now.

Note: These are approximate time frames. Allow for individual differences in puppies.

adult, the methods of teaching and the techniques we use in training basic behaviors are the same. After all, no dog, whether puppy or adult, likes harsh or inhumane methods. All creatures, however, respond favorably to gentle motivational methods and sincere praise and encouragement. Now let us get started.

HOUSE-TRAINING

You can train a puppy to relieve himself wherever you choose, but this must be somewhere suitable. You should bear in mind from the outset that when your puppy is old enough to go out in public places, any canine droppings must be removed at once. You will always have to carry with you a small plastic bag or "poop-scoop."

Outdoor training includes such surfaces as grass, soil and cement. Indoor training usually means training your dog to newspaper. When deciding on the surface and location that you will want your Coton to use, be sure it is going to be permanent. Training your dog to grass and then changing your mind a few months later is extremely difficult for both dog and owner.

Next, choose the command you will use each and every time you want your puppy to void. "Hurry up" and "Let's go" are examples of commands commonly used by dog owners. Get in the habit of giving the

TAKE THE LEAD
Do not carry your dog to his relief area. Lead him there on a leash or, better yet, encourage him to follow you to the spot. If you start carrying him to his spot, you might end up doing this routine forever and your dog will have the satisfaction of having trained *you*.

THE CLEAN LIFE

By providing sleeping and resting quarters that fit the dog, and offering frequent opportunities to relieve himself outside his quarters, the puppy quickly learns that the outdoors (or the newspaper if you are training him to paper) is the place to go when he needs to urinate or defecate. It also reinforces his innate desire to keep his sleeping quarters clean. This, in turn, helps develop the muscle control that will eventually produce a dog with clean living habits.

puppy your chosen relief command before you take him out. That way, when he becomes an adult, you will be able to determine if he wants to go out when you ask him. A confirmation will be signs of interest, such as wagging his tail, watching you intently, going to the door, etc.

PUPPY'S NEEDS

Your puppy needs to relieve himself after play periods, after each meal, after he has been sleeping and at any time he indicates that he is looking for a place to urinate or defecate. The urinary and intestinal tract muscles of very young puppies are not fully developed. Therefore, like human babies, puppies need to relieve themselves frequently.

Take your puppy out often—every hour for a ten-week-old, for example—and always immediately after sleeping and eating. The older the puppy, the less often he will need to relieve himself. Finally, as a mature healthy adult, he will require only three to five relief trips per day.

HOUSING

Since the types of housing and control you provide for your puppy have a direct relationship on the success of house-training, we consider the various aspects of both before we begin training.

Taking a new puppy home and turning him loose in your house can be compared to turning a child loose in an amusement park and telling the child that the place is all his! The sheer enormity of the place would be too much for him to handle. Instead, offer the puppy clearly defined areas where he can play, sleep, eat and live. A room of the house where the family gathers is the most obvious choice. Puppies are social animals and need to feel a part of the pack right from the start. Hearing your voice, watching you while you are doing things and smelling you nearby are all positive reinforcers that he is now a member of your pack. Usually a family room, the kitchen or a nearby adjoining breakfast area is ideal for providing safety and security for both puppy and owner.

Within the designated room, there should be a smaller area that the puppy can call his own. An alcove, a wire or fiberglass dog crate or a gated (not boarded!) corner from which he can view the activities of his new family will be fine. The size of the area or crate is the key factor here. The area must be large enough so that the puppy can lie down and stretch out, as well as stand up, without rubbing his head on the top. At the same time, it must be small enough so that he cannot relieve himself at one end and sleep at the other without coming into contact with his droppings. Dogs are, by nature, clean animals and will not remain close to their relief areas unless forced to do so. In those cases, they then become dirty dogs and usually remain that way for life.

The dog's designated area should contain clean bedding and a toy. Do not put food or water in the dog's crate during the house-

MEALTIME
Mealtime should be a peaceful time for your puppy. Do not put his food and water bowls in a high-traffic area in the house. For example, give him his own little corner of the kitchen where he can eat undisturbed and where he will not be underfoot. Do not allow small children or other family members to disturb the pup when he is eating.

training process, as eating and drinking will activate the pup's digestive processes and ultimately defeat your purpose, as well as make the puppy very uncomfortable between relief visits if he always has to "hold it." Once house-training is accomplished, water should always be made available in his crate or area, in a non-spill container.

CONTROL

By *control*, we mean helping the puppy to create a lifestyle pattern that will be compatible to that of his human pack *(you!)*. Just as we guide little children to learn our

THE SUCCESS METHOD

Success that comes by luck is usually short-lived. Success that comes by well-thought-out proven methods is often more easily achieved and permanent. This is the Success Method. It is designed to give you, the puppy owner, a simple yet proven way to help your puppy develop clean living habits and a feeling of security in his new environment.

6 Steps to Successful Crate Training

1 Tell the puppy "Crate time!" and place him in the crate with a small treat (a piece of cheese or half of a biscuit). Let him stay in the crate for five minutes while you are in the same room. Then release him and praise lavishly. Never release him when he is fussing. Wait until he is quiet before you let him out.

2 Repeat Step 1 several times a day.

3 The next day, place the puppy in the crate as before. Let him stay there for ten minutes. Do this several times.

4 Continue building time in five-minute increments until the puppy stays in his crate for 30 minutes with you in the room. Always take him to his relief area after prolonged periods in his crate.

5 Now go back to Step 1 and let the puppy stay in his crate for five minutes, this time while you are out of the room.

6 Once again, build crate time in five-minute increments with you out of the room. When the puppy will stay willingly in his crate (he may even fall asleep!) for 30 minutes with you out of the room, he will be ready to stay in it for several hours at a time.

way of life, we must show the puppy when it is time to play, eat, sleep, exercise and even entertain himself.

Your puppy should always sleep in his crate. He should also learn that, during times of household confusion and excessive human activity, such as at breakfast when family members are preparing for the day, he can play by himself in relative safety and comfort in his designated area. Each time you leave the puppy alone, he should understand exactly where he is to stay.

Puppies are chewers and cannot tell the difference between things like lamp and television cords, shoes, table legs, etc. Chewing into an electrical cord, for example, can be fatal to the puppy, while a shorted cord can start a fire in the house. If the puppy chews on the arm of the chair when he is alone, you will probably discipline him angrily when you get home. Thus, he makes the association that your coming home means he is going to be punished. (He will not remember chewing the chair and is incapable of making the association of the discipline with his naughty deed.) Accustoming the pup to his designated area not only keeps him safe but also avoids his engaging in destructive behaviors when you are not around.

Times of excitement, such as special occasions, family parties,

etc., can be fun for the puppy, providing that he can view the activities from the security of his designated area. He is not underfoot and he is not being fed all

HOUSE-TRAINING TIP

Most of all, be consistent. Always take your dog to the same location, always use the same command and always have the dog on lead when he is in his relief area, unless a fenced-in yard is available.

By following the Success Method, your puppy will be completely housebroken by the time his muscle and brain development reach maturity. Keep in mind that small breeds usually mature faster than large breeds, but all puppies should be trained by six months of age.

For some breeders, Cotons are a family affair! Such dedicated breeders provide the healthiest, most typical dogs as well as continued assistance to owners throughout the dogs' lives.

sorts of tidbits that will probably cause him stomach distress, yet he still feels a part of the fun.

SCHEDULE

A puppy should be taken to his relief area each time he is released from his designated area, after meals, after play sessions and when he first awakens in the morning (at age ten weeks, this can mean 5 a.m.!). The puppy will indicate that he's ready "to go" by circling or sniffing busily—do not

Clean habits apply to both dog and owner. Clean up after your dog, whether he's in his ex-pen, the backyard or a public place.

misinterpret these signs. For a puppy around ten weeks of age, a routine of taking him out every hour is necessary. As the puppy grows, he will be able to wait for longer periods of time.

Keep trips to his relief area short. Stay no more than five or six minutes and then return to the house. If he goes during that time, praise him lavishly and take him indoors immediately. If he does not, but he has an accident when you go back indoors, pick him up immediately, say "No! No!" and return to his relief area. Wait a few minutes, then return to the house again. Never hit a puppy or put his face in urine or excrement when he has had an accident!

Once indoors, put the puppy in his crate until you have had time to clean up his accident. Then, release him to the family area and watch him more closely than before. Chances are, his accident was a result of your not picking up his signal or waiting too long before offering him the opportunity to relieve himself. Never hold a grudge against the puppy for accidents.

Let the puppy learn that going outdoors means it is time to relieve himself, not to play. Once trained, he will be able to play indoors and out and still differentiate between the times for play versus the times for relief. Help him develop regular hours for naps, being alone, playing by

HOW MANY TIMES A DAY?

AGE	RELIEF TRIPS
To 14 weeks	10
14–22 weeks	8
22–32 weeks	6
Adulthood (dog stops growing)	4

These are estimates, of course, but they are a guide to the *minimum* number of opportunities a dog should have each day to relieve himself.

training is the answer for now and in the future.

In conclusion, a few key elements are really all you need for a successful house-training method—consistency, frequency, praise, control and supervision. By following these procedures with a normal, healthy puppy, you and the puppy will soon be past the stage of "accidents" and ready to move on to a clean and rewarding life together.

himself and just resting, all in his crate. Encourage him to entertain himself while you are busy with your activities. Let him learn that having you near is comforting, but it is not your main purpose in life to provide him with undivided attention. Each time you put your puppy in his own area, use the same command, whatever suits best. Soon he will run to his crate or special area when he hears you say those words.

Crate training provides safety for you, the puppy and the home. It also provides the puppy with a feeling of security, and that helps the puppy achieve self-confidence and clean habits. Remember that one of the primary ingredients in house-training your puppy is control. Regardless of your lifestyle, there will always be occasions when you will need to have a place where your dog can stay and be happy and safe. Crate

The crate is handy for travel as well as house-training. Although this Coton would rather be in the driver's seat, his crate is the safest place for him during car rides.

Before your Coton takes over the director's seat of your home and yard, be sure that he understands the rules of the household. Firm but fair treatment is best for every dog.

ROLES OF DISCIPLINE, REWARD AND PUNISHMENT

Discipline, training one to act in accordance with rules, brings order to life. It is as simple as that. Without discipline, particularly in a group society, chaos will reign supreme and the group will eventually perish. Humans and canines are social animals and need some form of discipline in order to function effectively. They must procure food, reproduce to keep their species going and protect their home base and their young. If there were no discipline in the lives of social animals, they would eventually die from starvation and/or predation by other stronger animals. In the case of

domestic canines, discipline in their lives is needed in order for them to understand how their pack (you and other family members) functions and how they must act in order to survive.

A large humane society in a highly populated area recently surveyed dog owners regarding their satisfaction with their relationships with their dogs. People who had trained their dogs were 75% more satisfied with their pets than those who had never trained their dogs.

Dr. Edward Thorndike, a

THE STUDENT'S STRESS TEST

During training sessions, you must be able to recognize signs of stress in your dog such as:
- tucking his tail between his legs
- lowering his head
- shivering or trembling
- standing completely still or running away
- panting and/or salivating
- avoiding eye contact
- flattening his ears back
- urinating submissively
- rolling over and lifting a leg
- grinning or baring teeth
- aggression when restrained

If your four-legged student displays these signs, he may just be nervous or intimidated. The training session may have been too lengthy, with not enough praise and affirmation. Stop for the day and try again tomorrow.

KEEP SMILING

Never train your dog, puppy or adult, when you are angry or in a sour mood. Dogs are very sensitive to human feelings, especially anger, and if your dog senses that you are angry or upset, he will connect your anger with his training and learn to resent or fear his training sessions.

noted psychologist, established *Thorndike's Theory of Learning*, which states that a behavior that results in a pleasant event tends to be repeated. Furthermore, it concludes that a behavior that results in an unpleasant event tends not to be repeated. It is this theory upon which training methods are based today. For example, if you manipulate a dog to perform a specific behavior and reward him for doing it, he is likely to do it again because he enjoyed the end result.

Occasionally, punishment, a penalty inflicted for an offense, is necessary. The best type of punishment often comes from an outside source. For example, a child is told not to touch the stove because he may get burned. He disobeys and touches the stove. In doing so, he receives a burn. From that time on, he respects the heat of the stove and avoids contact with it. Therefore, a behavior that results in an unpleasant event tends not to be repeated.

A good example of a dog's learning the hard way is the dog who chases the house cat. He is told many times to leave the cat alone, yet he persists in teasing the cat. Then, one day, the dog begins chasing the cat but the cat turns and swipes a claw across the dog's face, leaving the dog with a painful gash on his nose. The final result is that the dog stops chasing the cat.

TRAINING EQUIPMENT

COLLAR AND LEAD

For a Coton, the collar and lead that you use for training must be one with which you are easily able to work, not too heavy for the dog and perfectly safe.

Put the lead on your puppy and proceed to take a very short walk. At first he may resist, but with a little encouragement (and a tug or two) he'll comply. Soon he won't even know the lead is there.

Show dogs must
be tolerant of the
judge's handling
of their mouth.
Practice this at
home.

Show dogs must be tolerant of the judge's handling of their mouth. Practice this at home.

PRACTICE MAKES PERFECT!

- Have training lessons with your dog every day in several short segments—three to five times a day for a few minutes at a time is ideal.
- Do not have long practice sessions. The dog will become easily bored.
- Never practice when you are tired, ill, worried or in an otherwise negative mood. This will transmit to the dog and may have an adverse effect on his performance.

  Think fun, short and above all *positive!* End each session on a high note, rather than a failed exercise, and make sure to give a lot of praise. Enjoy the training and help your dog enjoy it, too.

TREATS

Have a bag of treats on hand; something nutritious and easy to swallow works best. Use a soft treat, a chunk of cheese or a piece of cooked chicken rather than a dry biscuit. By the time the dog has finished chewing a dry treat, he will forget why he is being rewarded in the first place!

As a sidebar, using food rewards will not teach a dog to beg at the table—the only way to teach a dog to beg at the table is to give him food from the table. In training, rewarding the dog with a food treat will help him associate praise and the treats with learning new behaviors that obviously please his owner.

TRAINING BEGINS: ASK THE DOG A QUESTION

In order to teach your dog anything, you must first get his attention. After all, he cannot learn anything if he is looking away from you with his mind on something else.

To get your dog's attention, ask him "School?" and immediately walk over to him and give him a treat as you tell him "Good dog." Wait a minute or two and repeat the routine, this time with a treat in your hand as you approach within a foot of the dog. Do not go directly to him, but stop about a foot short of him and hold out the treat as you ask "School?" He will see you approaching with a treat in your hand and most likely begin walking toward you. As you meet, give him the treat and praise again.

The third time, ask the question, have a treat in your hand and walk only a short distance toward the dog so that he must walk almost all the way to you. As he reaches you, give him the treat and praise again.

By this time, the dog will probably be getting the idea that if he pays attention to you, especially when you ask that question, it will pay off in treats and enjoyable activities for him. In other words, he learns that "school" means doing great things with you that are fun and that result in positive attention for him.

Remember that the dog does not understand your verbal language; he only recognizes sounds. Your question translates to a series of sounds for him, and those sounds become the signal to go to you and pay attention. The dog learns that if he does this, he will get to interact with you plus receive treats and praise.

THE BASIC COMMANDS

TEACHING SIT

Now that you have the dog's attention, attach his lead and hold it in your left hand, and hold a food treat in your right hand. Place your food hand at the dog's nose and let him lick the treat but not take it from you. Say "Sit" and slowly raise your food hand from in front of the dog's nose up over his head so that he is looking at the ceiling. As he bends his head upward, he will have to bend his knees to maintain his balance. As he bends his knees, he will assume a sit position. At that point, release the food treat and praise lavishly with comments such as "Good dog! Good sit!," etc. Remember to always praise enthusiastically, because dogs relish verbal praise from their owners and feel so proud of themselves whenever

Teaching the basic commands always starts with the sit lesson. This is the easiest command to teach a dog and provides your curriculum with a positive, successful lesson to fall back on. End every lesson with a successful command.

DOUBLE JEOPARDY
A dog in jeopardy never lies down. He stays alert on his feet because instinct tells him that he may have to run away or fight for his survival. Therefore, if a dog feels threatened or anxious, he will not lie down. Consequently, it is important to keep the dog calm and relaxed as he learns the down exercise.

they accomplish a behavior.

You will not use food forever in getting the dog to obey your commands. Food is only used to teach new behaviors and, once the dog knows what you want when you give a specific

command, you will wean him off the food treats but still maintain the verbal praise. After all, you will always have your voice with you, and there will be many times when you have no food rewards but expect the dog to obey.

TEACHING DOWN
Teaching the down exercise is easy when you understand how the dog perceives the down position, and it is very difficult when you do not. Dogs perceive the down position as a submissive one; therefore, teaching the down exercise by using a forceful method can sometimes make the dog develop such a fear of the down that he either runs away when you say "Down" or he attempts to snap at the person who tries to force him down.

Have the dog sit close alongside your left leg, facing in the same direction as you are. Hold the lead in your left hand and a food treat in your right. Now place your left hand lightly on the top of the dog's shoulders where they meet above the spinal cord. Do not push down on the dog's shoulders; simply rest your left hand there so you can guide the dog to lie down close to your left leg rather than to swing away from your side when he drops.

Now place the food hand at the dog's nose, say "Down" very softly (almost a whisper) and slowly lower the food hand to the dog's front feet. When the food hand reaches the floor, begin moving it forward along the floor in front of the dog. Keep talking softly to the dog, saying things like, "Do you want this treat? You can do this, good dog." Your reassuring tone of voice will help calm the dog as he tries to follow the food hand in order to get the treat.

When the dog's elbows touch the floor, release the food and praise softly. Try to get the dog to maintain that down position for several seconds before you let him sit up again. The goal here is to get the dog to settle down and not feel threatened in the down position.

TEACHING STAY

It is easy to teach the dog to stay in either a sit or a down position. Again, we use food and praise during the teaching process as we help the dog to understand exactly what it is that we are expecting him to do.

To teach the sit/stay, start with the dog sitting on your left side as before and hold the lead in your left hand. Have a food treat in your right hand and place your food hand at the dog's nose. Say "Stay" and step out on your right foot to stand directly in front of the dog, toe to toe, as he licks and nibbles the treat. Be sure to keep his head facing upward to maintain the sit position. Count to five

and then swing around to stand next to the dog again with him on your left. As soon as you get back to the original position, release

CONSISTENCY PAYS OFF

Dogs need consistency in their feeding schedule, exercise and relief visits, and in the verbal commands you use. If you use "Stay" on Monday and "Stay here, please" on Tuesday, you will confuse your dog. Don't demand perfect behavior during training sessions and then let him have the run of the house the rest of the day. Above all, lavish praise on your pet consistently every time he does something right. The more he feels he is pleasing you, the more willing he will be to learn.

Execute every lesson with your Coton on his lead before attempting to teach the command off-lead. In time, the dog will be reliable enough to execute the command without the lead, but you should only do this in a securely fenced area.

THE GOLDEN RULE

The golden rule of dog training is simple. For each "question" (command), there is only one correct answer (reaction). One command = one reaction. Keep practicing the command until the dog reacts correctly without hesitating. Be repetitive but not monotonous. Dogs get bored just as people do!

the food and praise lavishly.

To teach the down/stay, do the down as previously described. As soon as the dog lies down, say "Stay" and step out on your right foot just as you did in the sit/stay. Count to five and then return to stand beside the dog with him on your left side. Release the treat and praise as always.

Within a week or ten days, you can begin to add a bit of distance between you and your dog when you leave him. When you do, use your left hand open with the palm facing the dog as a stay signal, much the same as the hand signal a police officer uses to stop traffic at an intersection. Hold the food treat in your right hand as before, but this time the food will not be touching the dog's nose. He will watch the food hand and quickly learn that he is going to get that treat as soon as you return to his side.

When you can stand 3 feet away from your dog for 30 seconds, you can then begin building time and distance in both stays. Eventually, the dog can be expected to remain in the stay position for prolonged periods of time until you return to him or call him to you. Always praise lavishly when he stays.

TEACHING COME

If you make teaching "come" an exciting experience, you should never have a "student" that does not love the game or that fails to come when called. The secret, it seems, is never to teach the word "come."

At times when an owner most wants his dog to come when called, the owner is likely to be upset or anxious and he allows these feelings to come through in the tone of his voice when he calls his dog. Hearing that desperation in his owner's voice, the dog fears the results of going to him and therefore either disobeys outright or runs in the opposite direction. The secret, therefore, is

to teach the dog a game and, when you want him to come to you, simply play the game. It is practically a no-fail solution!

To begin, have several members of your family take a few food treats and each go into a different room in the house. Everyone takes turns calling the dog, and each person should celebrate the dog's finding him with a treat and lots of happy praise. When a person calls the dog, he is actually inviting the dog to find him and to get a treat as a reward for "winning."

A few turns of the "Where are you?" game and the dog will understand that everyone is playing the game and that each person has a big celebration awaiting the dog's success at locating him or her. Once the dog learns to love the game, simply calling out "Where are you?" will bring him

Show dogs are often taught the stand command, which is necessary for the dog when he is being exhibited. "Stand" indicates that the dog should remain in a standing position without moving while the judge reviews him.

"COME"... BACK

Never call your dog to come to you for a correction or scold him when he reaches you. That is the quickest way to turn a come command into "Go away fast!" Dogs think only in the present tense, and your dog will connect the scolding with coming to you, not with the misbehavior of a few moments earlier.

HEELING IN THE RING

When showing a dog, the dog should at all times be kept at heel on the side facing the judge. Since the Coton de Tuléar is not a working dog, keeping him on your left side is not a necessity. If the judge, for example, stands outside the ring, it is fine to guide the Coton on your right side.

running from wherever he is when he hears that all-important question.

The come command is recognized as one of the most important things to teach a dog, but there are trainers who work with thousands of dogs and never use the actual word "come." Yet these dogs will race to respond to a person who uses the dog's name followed by "Where are you?" For example, a woman has a 12-year-old companion dog who went blind, but who never fails to locate her owner when asked, "Where are you?"

Children, in particular, love to play this game with their dogs. Children can hide in smaller places like a shower or bathtub, behind a bed or under a table. The dog needs to work a little bit harder to find these hiding places, but, when he does, he loves to celebrate with a treat and a tussle with a favorite youngster.

TEACHING HEEL

Heeling means that the dog walks beside the owner without pulling. It takes time and patience on the owner's part to succeed at teaching the dog that he (the owner) will not proceed unless the dog is walking calmly beside him. Neither pulling out ahead on the lead nor lagging behind is acceptable.

Begin by holding the lead in your left hand as the dog sits beside your left leg. Move the loop end of the lead to your right hand, but keep your left hand short on the lead so that it keeps the dog in close next to you. Say "Heel" and step forward on your left foot. Keep the dog close to you and take three steps. Stop and have the dog sit next to you in what we now call the heel position. Praise verbally, but do not touch the dog. Hesitate a moment and begin again with "Heel," taking three steps and stopping, at which point the dog is told to sit again.

Your goal here is to have the dog walk those three steps without pulling on the lead. Once he will walk calmly beside you for three steps without pulling, increase the number of steps you take to five. When he will walk politely beside you while you take five steps, you can increase the length of your walk to ten steps. Keep increasing the length of your stroll until the dog will walk quietly beside you without pulling as long as you want him to heel. When you stop heeling, indicate to the dog that the exercise is over by verbally praising as you pet him and say, "OK, good dog." The "OK" is used as a release word, meaning that the exercise is finished and the dog is free to relax.

If you are dealing with a dog who insists on pulling you around, simply "put on your brakes" and stand your ground until the dog realizes that the two of you are not going anywhere until he is beside you and moving at your pace, not his. It may take some time just standing there to convince the dog that you are the leader and that you will be the one to decide on the direction and speed of your travel.

Each time the dog looks up at you or slows down to give a slack lead between the two of you, quietly praise him and say, "Good heel. Good dog." Eventually, the dog will begin to respond and within a few days he will be walking politely beside you without pulling on the lead. At first, the training sessions should be kept short and very positive; soon the dog will be able to walk nicely with you for increasingly longer distances. Remember also to give the dog free time and the opportunity to run and play when you have finished heel practice.

WEANING OFF FOOD IN TRAINING

Food is used in training new behaviors. Once the dog understands what behavior goes with a specific command, it is time to start weaning him off the food treats. At first, give a treat after each exercise. Then, start to give a treat only after every other exercise. Mix up the times when you offer a food reward and the times

HEELING WELL
Teach your dog to heel in an enclosed area. Once you think the dog will obey reliably and you want to attempt advanced obedience exercises such as off-lead heeling, test him in a fenced-in area so he cannot run away.

when you only offer praise so that the dog will never know when he is going to receive both food and praise and when he is going to receive only praise. This is called a variable-ratio reward system. It proves successful because there is always the chance that the owner will produce a treat, so the dog never stops trying for that reward. No matter what, *always* give verbal praise.

TRAINING FOR THE SHOW RING

Presenting a dog properly in a show ring requires quite a bit of effort on the part of the owner. The dog has to be trained to the routine of the ring, and there are many things for you to learn your-

Show training takes practice outside the ring. Even though exhibiting dogs looks simple to the spectator, it takes practice to teach the dog to stand, gait and behave while in the ring.

self. If you wish to show your Coton on a competitive level, a number of steps must be taken when the dog is still quite young. There are a multitude of details to attend to before a handler and dog develop the necessary teamwork to conquer the show ring. The first step would certainly be to teach the dog to walk on lead properly, which already should be part of your basic training. Just remember that, during his training, don't be too demanding of your young pup.

Another thing to consider is that, in the case of a long-haired dog such as the Coton de Tuléar, you must know how to ensure that the dog remains perfectly styled in the ring, despite moving the dog on and off the judging table and the judge's touching the dog. Any adjustments can only be made in a flash, if even at all possible. The judges always have their eyes on the dogs in the ring, and you must be discreet about making any adjustments. "Showy" means that the Coton has to present himself at his very best.

In single presentations, the dog is usually moved in a pattern that allows the judge to evaluate his gait from behind, from the side and from the front. For the subsequent evaluation on the judging table, the dog has to stay standing nicely ("stacked"). It is required that the dog looks at the judge during the entire process. In order to emphasize the outline of the dog in a favorable manner, you should ensure that the long hair of the tail falls to the side of the dog that faces the judge. The judge will examine the dog's structure and make certain that he conforms to the breed standard. By pulling up the lips, the judge will check for possible faults in the bite. The Coton will be required to endure all of the hands-on evaluation of the coat and overall appearance, and even of the testicles in the case of a male dog, with friendly patience.

OBEDIENCE SCHOOL

Taking your dog to an obedience school and practicing with him at home is a very worthwhile investment of time and money. You will enjoy the benefits for the lifetime of your dog and you will have the opportunity to meet people who have similar expectations for companion dogs.

Before the show, the dog has to be bathed and brushed with extra care so that he looks his best in the ring, but this is not a breed that requires fancy grooming and sculpting.

OTHER COMPETITIVE EVENTS AND ACTIVITIES

OBEDIENCE

It is a good idea to enroll in an obedience class if one is available in your area. Many areas have dog clubs that offer basic obedience training as well as preparatory classes for obedience competition. There are also local dog trainers who offer similar classes.

At obedience shows and trials, dogs can earn titles at various levels of competition. The beginning levels of obedience competition include basic behaviors such as sit, down, heel, etc. The more advanced levels of competition include jumping, retrieving, scent discrimination and signal work. The advanced levels require a dog and owner to put a lot of time and effort into their training. The titles that can be earned at these levels of competition are very prestigious.

AGILITY: WHAT FUN MEANS TO THE COTON

For many, owners and dogs alike, fun means to enjoy some kind of activity or sport. Responding to this need, the sport of agility was introduced at the Crufts Dog Show in England in 1977. Training for agility is most suitable for enhancing a dog's coordination, dexterity and endurance, while being enjoyable for the dog. Agility training means an opportunity to face mental and physical challenges, in the form of learning how to negotiate various types of obstacles, that help him develop his senses, keep him fit and provide him with more skills. This can be an especially refreshing change for a dog living in a city apartment. The dog's positive temperament traits are enhanced and his ability to concentrate is strengthened. Agility training also solidifies the bond between owner and dog as they form a team. In an agility trial, the handler and dog progress through the course together as the handler uses commands to help guide the dog through the set of obstacles.

Despite the breed's small size, the Coton is very much able to participate in this sport. He competes enthusiastically and has no problems in managing a course with obstacles that have been adjusted proportionately to his height. The Coton de Tuléar is an alert participant that enjoys jumping and climbing. In fact, his ever-driving motivation to please his owner makes him a very good agility dog. Obviously, the exercises must not pose a danger to the dog, and dogs should not

> **TRAINING RULES**
> If you want to be successful in training your dog, you have four rules to obey yourself:
> 1. Develop an understanding of how a dog thinks.
> 2. Do not blame the dog for lack of communication.
> 3. Define your dog's personality and act accordingly.
> 4. Have patience and be consistent.

begin agility training until at least 12 months of age. They are not eligible to compete earlier than that. And, of course, agility should only be pursued if the individual dog enjoys it.

Owners of Cotons who seriously consider participating with their dogs in agility trials should lay a proper foundation by teaching the aforementioned basic commands in puppyhood. The dog's obedience will make progressing to learning the agility exercises much easier, and obedience is one of the most important precursors for this sport. Agility has become very popular among owners and dogs, and attracts dogs of all breeds and sizes.

ACTIVITIES AT HOME
Whether a dog is trained in the structured environment of a class or alone with his owner at home, there are many activities that can bring fun and rewards to both

owner and dog once they have mastered basic control. For example, teaching the dog to help out around the home, in the yard or on the farm provides great satisfaction to both dog and owner. In addition, the dog's help makes life a little easier for his owner and raises his stature as a valued companion to his family. It helps give the dog a purpose by occupying his mind and providing an outlet for his energy.

Hiking is an exciting and healthy activity that the dog can be taught without assistance from more than his owner. The exercise of walking and climbing is good

OPEN MINDS
Dogs are as different from each other as people are. What works for one dog may not work for another. Have an open mind. If one method of training is unsuccessful, try another.

for man and dog alike, and the bond that they develop together is priceless. Your Coton may even carry along his own little pack with him, but be careful not to make it too heavy. The rule of thumb with any dog is never to expect him to carry more than one-sixth of his body weight.

Many Cotons are talented swimmers and take to the water quite naturally. The Bichon breeds are related to the water dogs and prove to be superb swimmers if introduced to the water properly.

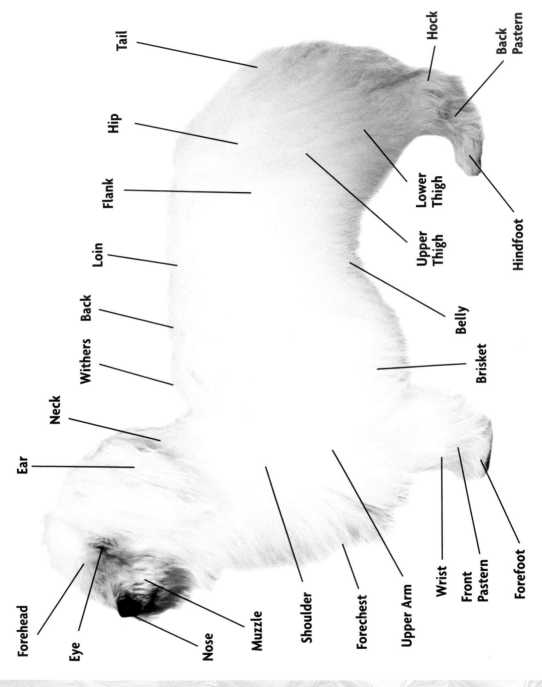

Tail

Hock

Back
Pastern

Hip

Lower
Thigh

Flank

Upper
Thigh

Loin

Hindfoot

Back

Withers

Belly

Neck

Brisket

Ear

Forehead

Eye

Nose

Muzzle

Shoulder

Forechest

Upper Arm

Wrist

Front
Pastern

Forefoot

PHYSICAL STRUCTURE OF THE COTON DE TULÉAR

Dogs suffer from many of the same physical illnesses as people and might even share many of the same psychological problems. Since people usually know more about human diseases than canine maladies, many of the terms used in this chapter will be familiar but not necessarily those used by vets. For example, we will use the familiar term *x-ray* instead of *radiograph*. We will also use the familiar term *symptoms*, even though dogs don't have symptoms, which are verbal descriptions of something the patient feels or observes himself that he regards as abnormal. Dogs have *clinical signs* since they cannot speak, so we have to look for these clinical signs…but we still use the term *symptoms* in the book.

Medicine is a constantly changing art, with of course scientific input as well. Things alter as we learn more and more about basic sciences such as genetics and biochemistry, and have use of more sophisticated imaging techniques like Computer Aided Tomography (CAT scans) or Magnetic Resonance Imaging (MRI scans). There is academic dispute about many canine maladies, so different vets treat them in different ways. For example, some vets place a greater emphasis on surgical techniques than others.

SELECTING A VET

Your selection of a vet should be based on personal recommendation for his skills with small animals, especially dogs, and, if possible, especially the Coton or similar breeds. If the vet is based nearby, it will be helpful because you might have an emergency or need to make multiple visits for treatments.

All vets are licensed and should be capable of dealing with routine medical issues such as infections, injuries and the promotion of health (for example, by vaccination). If the problem affecting your dog is more complex, your vet will refer your pet to someone with a more detailed knowledge of what is wrong. This will usually be a specialist who concentrates in the field relevant to your dog's problem, e.g., veterinary dermatology, veterinary ophthalmology, veterinary oncology and so on.

Veterinary procedures are very costly and, as the treatments avail-

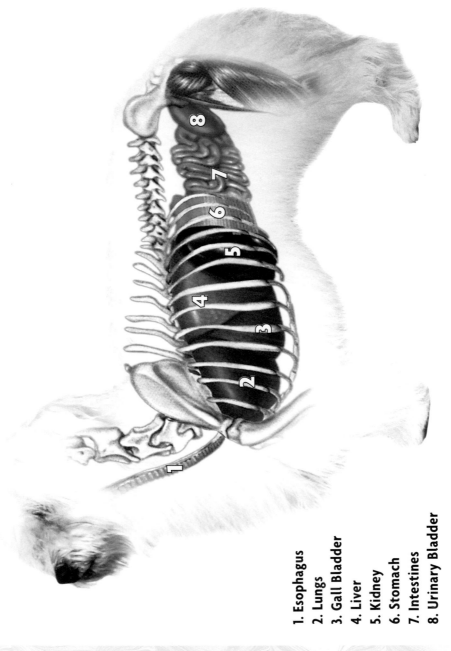

1. Esophagus
2. Lungs
3. Gall Bladder
4. Liver
5. Kidney
6. Stomach
7. Intestines
8. Urinary Bladder

INTERNAL ORGANS OF THE COTON DE TULÉAR

able improve, they are going to become more expensive. It is quite acceptable to discuss matters of cost with your vet; if there is more than one treatment option, cost may be a factor in deciding which route to take.

PREVENTATIVE MEDICINE

It is much easier, less costly and more effective to practice preventative medicine than to fight bouts of illness and disease. Properly bred puppies of all breeds come from parents that were selected based upon their genetic-disease profiles. The puppies' mother should have been vaccinated, free of all internal and external parasites and properly nourished. For those reasons, a visit to the vet who cared for the dam is recommended if at all possible. The dam passes disease resistance to her puppies, which should last from eight to ten weeks. Unfortunately, she can also pass on parasites and infection. This is why knowledge about her health is useful in learning more about the health of the puppies.

WEANING TO BRINGING PUPPY HOME

Puppies should be weaned by the time they are two months old. A puppy that remains for at least eight weeks with his mother and littermates usually adapts better to other dogs and people later in his life. Sometimes new owners have their puppy examined by a vet

Breakdown of Veterinary Income by Category

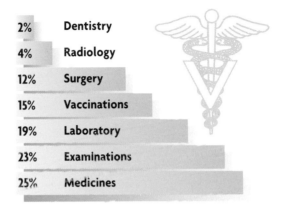

2%	Dentistry
4%	Radiology
12%	Surgery
15%	Vaccinations
19%	Laboratory
23%	Examinations
25%	Medicines

immediately, which is a good idea unless the puppy is overtired by a long journey, in which case an appointment should be arranged for the next day or so.

The puppy will have his teeth examined and have his skeletal conformation and general health checked prior to certification by the vet. Puppies in certain breeds have problems with their kneecaps, cataracts and other eye problems, heart murmurs and undescended testicles. Your vet may also have training in temperament evaluation. The vet will set up a schedule for your Coton's vaccinations program at the first visit as well.

VACCINATIONS

Most vaccinations are given by injection and should only be given by a vet, though experienced breeders may vaccinate their own

A typical vet's income, categorized according to services performed. This survey dealt with small-animal (pets) practices.

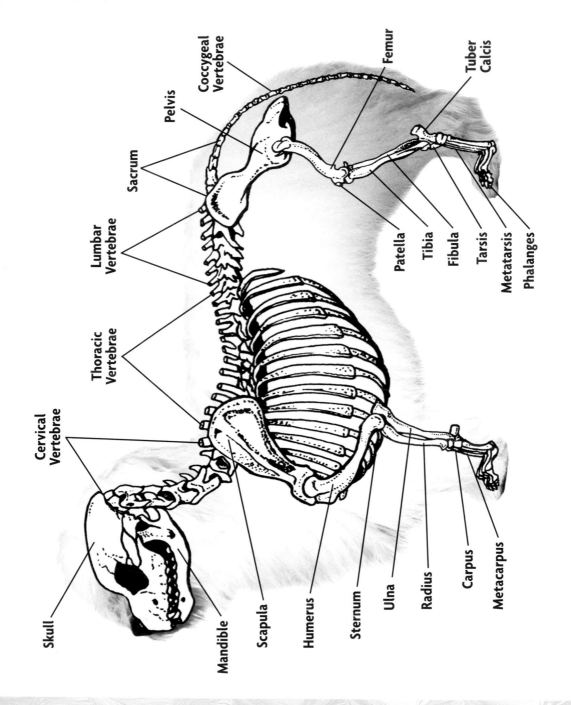

Coccygeal Vertebrae

Femur

Tuber Calcis

Pelvis

Sacrum

Patella

Tibia

Fibula

Tarsis

Metatarsis

Phalanges

Lumbar Vertebrae

Thoracic Vertebrae

Cervical Vertebrae

Skull

Mandible

Scapula

Humerus

Sternum

Ulna

Radius

Carpus

Metacarpus

SKELETAL STRUCTURE OF THE COTON DE TULÉAR

pups. Both he and you should keep a record of the date of the injection, the identification of the vaccine and the amount given. Some vets give a first vaccination at six weeks, but most dog breeders prefer the course not to commence until about eight weeks because of the risk of interaction with the antibodies produced by the mother. The vaccination timetable is usually based on a two- to four-week cycle. You must take your vet's advice as to when to vaccinate, as this may differ according to the vaccine used.

The usual vaccines contain immunizing doses of several different viruses such as distemper, parvovirus, parainfluenza and hepatitis. There are other vaccines available when the puppy is at risk. You should rely upon professional advice. This is especially true for the booster immunizations. Most vaccination programs require a booster when the puppy is a year old and once a year thereafter. In some cases, circumstances may require more or less frequent immunizations.

Canine cough, more formally known as tracheobronchitis, is immunized against with a vaccine that is sprayed into the dog's nostrils. Canine cough is usually

HEALTH AND VACCINATION SCHEDULE

Age in Weeks:	6th	8th	10th	12th	14th	16th	20-24th	52nd
Worm Control	✔	✔	✔	✔	✔	✔	✔	
Neutering							✔	
Heartworm		✔		✔		✔	✔	
Parvovirus	✔		✔		✔		✔	✔
Distemper		✔		✔		✔		✔
Hepatitis		✔		✔		✔		✔
Leptospirosis								✔
Parainfluenza	✔		✔		✔			✔
Dental Examination		✔					✔	✔
Complete Physical		✔					✔	✔
Coronavirus				✔			✔	✔
Canine Cough	✔							
Hip Dysplasia								✔
Rabies							✔	

Vaccinations are not instantly effective. It takes about two weeks for the dog's immune system to develop antibodies. Most vaccinations require annual booster shots. Your vet should guide you in this regard.

included in routine vaccination, but it is often not as effective as the vaccines for other major diseases.

FIVE MONTHS TO ONE YEAR OF AGE
Unless you intend to breed or show your dog, neutering or spaying the puppy is recommended. Discuss all aspects of the procedure with your vet. Neutering/spaying has proven to be extremely beneficial to male and female dogs, respectively. Besides eliminating the possibility of preg-

nancy and pyometra in bitches and testicular cancer in males, it greatly reduces the risk of (but does not prevent) breast cancer in bitches and prostate cancer in male dogs.

Your vet should provide your puppy with a thorough dental evaluation at six months of age, ascertaining whether all of the permanent teeth have erupted properly. A home dental-care regimen should be initiated at six months, including brushing weekly and providing good dental

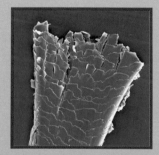
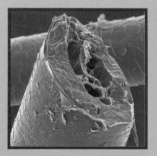

Normal hairs of a dog enlarged 200 times original size. The cuticle (outer covering) is clean and healthy. Unlike human hair that grows from the base, a dog's hair also grows from the end. Damaged hairs and split ends, illustrated above.

SCANNING ELECTRON MICROGRAPHS BY DR. DENNIS KUNKEL, UNIVERSITY OF HAWAII.

DISEASE REFERENCE CHART

	What is it?	What causes it?	Symptoms
Leptospirosis	Severe disease that affects the internal organs; can be spread to people.	A bacterium, which is often carried by rodents, that enters through mucous membranes and spreads quickly throughout the body.	Range from fever, vomiting and loss of appetite in less severe cases to shock, irreversible kidney damage and possibly death in most severe cases.
Rabies	Potentially deadly virus that infects warm-blooded mammals.	Bite from a carrier of the virus, mainly wild animals.	1st stage: dog exhibits change in behavior, fear. 2nd stage: dog's behavior becomes more aggressive. 3rd stage: loss of coordination, trouble with bodily functions.
Parvovirus	Highly contagious virus, potentially deadly.	Ingestion of the virus, which is usually spread through the feces of infected dogs.	Most common: severe diarrhea. Also vomiting, fatigue, lack of appetite.
Canine cough	Contagious respiratory infection.	Combination of types of bacteria and virus. Most common: *Bordetella bronchiseptica* bacteria and parainfluenza virus.	Chronic cough.
Distemper	Disease primarily affecting respiratory and nervous system.	Virus that is related to the human measles virus.	Mild symptoms such as fever, lack of appetite and mucus secretion progress to evidence of brain damage, "hard pad."
Hepatitis	Virus primarily affecting the liver.	Canine adenovirus type I (CAV-I). Enters system when dog breathes in particles.	Lesser symptoms include listlessness, diarrhea, vomiting. More severe symptoms include "blue-eye" (clumps of virus in eye).
Coronavirus	Virus resulting in digestive problems.	Virus is spread through infected dog's feces.	Stomach upset evidenced by lack of appetite, vomiting, diarrhea.

devices (such as hard plastic or nylon bones). Regular dental care promotes healthy teeth, fresh breath and a longer life.

DOGS OLDER THAN ONE YEAR

Continue to visit the vet at least once a year. There is no such disease as "old age," but bodily functions do change with age. The eyes and ears are no longer as efficient. Liver, kidney and intestinal functions often decline. Proper dietary changes, recommended by your vet, can make life more pleasant for your aging Coton de Tuléar and you.

SKIN PROBLEMS

Vets are consulted by dog owners for skin problems more than for any other group of diseases or maladies. A dog's skin is as sensitive, if not more so, than human skin, and both suffer from almost the same ailments (though the occurrence of acne in most dogs is rare). For this reason, veterinary dermatology has developed into a specialty practiced by many vets.

Since many skin problems have visual symptoms that are almost identical, it requires the skill of an experienced veterinary dermatologist to identify and cure many of the more severe skin disorders. Pet shops sell many treatments for skin problems, but most of the treatments are directed at symptoms and not at the underlying problem(s). If your dog is suffering from a skin disorder, you should seek professional assistance as quickly as possible. As with all diseases, the earlier a problem is identified and treated, the more likely it is that the cure will be successful.

HEREDITARY SKIN DISORDERS
Veterinary dermatologists are currently researching a number of skin disorders that are believed to have a hereditary

basis. These inherited diseases are transmitted by both parents, who appear (phenotypically) normal but have a recessive gene for the disease, meaning that they carry, but are not affected by, the disease. These diseases pose serious problems to breeders because in some instances there are no methods of identifying carriers. Often the secondary diseases associated with these skin conditions are even more debilitating than the skin disorders themselves, including cancers and respiratory problems.

Among the hereditary skin disorders, for which the mode of inheritance is known, are acrodermatitis, cutaneous asthenia (Ehlers-Danlos syndrome), sebaceous adenitis, cyclic hematopoiesis, dermatomyositis, IgA deficiency, color dilution alopecia and nodular dermatofibrosis. Some of these disorders are limited to one or two breeds, while others affect a large number of breeds. All inherited diseases must be diagnosed and treated by a veterinary specialist.

PARASITE BITES
Many of us are allergic to insect bites. The bites itch, erupt and may even become infected. Dogs have the same reaction to fleas, ticks and/or mites. When an insect lands on you, you have the chance to whisk it away with your hand. Unfortunately, when a

> **DENTAL HEALTH**
> A dental examination is in order when the dog is between six months and one year of age so that any permanent teeth that have erupted incorrectly can be corrected. It is important to begin a brushing routine at home, using a toothbrush made for dogs and a specially formulated canine toothpaste. Durable nylon and safe edible chews should be a part of your puppy's arsenal for good health, good teeth and pleasant breath. The vast majority of dogs three to four years old and older has diseases of the gums from lack of dental attention. Using the various types of dental chews can be very effective in controlling dental plaque.

dog is bitten by a flea, tick or mite, he can only scratch it away or bite it. By the time the dog has been bitten, the parasite has done some of its damage. It may also have laid eggs, which will cause further problems in the near future. The itching from parasite bites is probably due to the saliva injected into the site when the parasite sucks the dog's blood.

AIRBORNE ALLERGIES

Just as humans suffer from hay fever during the pollinating season, many dogs suffer from the same allergies. When the pollen count is high, your dog might suffer, but don't expect him to sneeze and have a runny nose as a human would. Dogs react to pollen allergies in the same way they react to fleas—they scratch and bite themselves. Dogs, like humans, can be tested for allergens. Discuss the testing with your vet.

AUTO-IMMUNE ILLNESSES

An auto-immune illness is one in which the immune system over-acts and does not recognize parts of the affected person; rather, the immune system starts to react as if these parts were foreign and need to be destroyed. An example is rheumatoid arthritis, which occurs when the body does not recognize the joints, thus leading to a very painful and damaging reaction in the joints. This has

nothing to do with age, so can occur in children and young dogs. The wear-and-tear arthritis of the older person or dog is osteoarthritis.

Lupus is an auto-immune disease that affects dogs as well as people. It can take variable forms, affecting the kidneys, bones and the skin. It can be fatal, so is treated with steroids, which can themselves have very significant side effects. The steroids calm down the allergic reaction to the body's tissues, which helps the lupus, but the steroids also decrease the body's reaction to real foreign substances such as bacteria, and they also thin the skin and bone.

FOOD PROBLEMS

FOOD ALLERGIES

Some dogs can be allergic to many foods that are best-sellers and highly recommended by breeders and vets. Changing the brand of food that you buy may not eliminate the problem if the element to which the dog is allergic is contained in the new brand.

Recognizing a food allergy in a dog can be difficult. Humans often have rashes when they eat foods to which they are allergic, or have swelling of the lips or eyes. Dogs do not usually develop rashes, but react in the same way as they do to an

PROPER DIET
Feeding your dog properly is very important. An incorrect diet could affect the dog's health, behavior and nervous system, possibly making a normal dog into an aggressive one. Its most visible effects are to the skin and coat, but internal organs are similarly affected.

airborne or bite allergy—they itch, scratch and bite. While pollen allergies are usually seasonal, food allergies are year-round problems.

TREATING FOOD ALLERGY
Diagnosis of food allergy is based on a two- to four-week dietary trial with a home-cooked diet fed to the exclusion of all other foods. The diet should consist of boiled rice or potato with a source of protein that the dog has never eaten before, such as fresh or frozen fish, lamb or even something as exotic as pheasant. Water has to be the only drink, and it is really important that no other foods are fed during this trial. If the dog's condition improves, you will need to try the original diet once again to see if the itching resumes. If it does, then this confirms the diagnosis that the dog is allergic to his original diet. The treatment is long-term feeding of something that

does not distress the dog's skin, which may be in the form of one of the commercially available hypoallergenic diets or the home-made diet that you created for the allergy trial.

FOOD INTOLERANCE
Food intolerance is the inability of the dog to completely digest certain foods. This occurs because the dog does not have the chemicals necessary to digest some foodstuffs. These chemicals are called enzymes. All puppies have the enzymes necessary to digest canine milk, but some dogs do not have the enzymes to digest a very different form of milk that is commonly found in human households—milk from cows. In such dogs, drinking cows' milk results in loose bowels, stomach pains and the passage of gas.

Dogs often do not have the enzymes to digest soy or other beans. The treatment is to exclude the foodstuffs that upset your Coton's digestion.

HEREDITARY EYE DISEASES IN THE COTON
Hereditary eye disorders concern every responsible breeder and owner of the Coton. Breeders must test their breeding stock before matings take place to ensure that they only breed dogs that have been cleared of any hereditary disorder. Yearly eye

Number-One Killer Disease in Dogs: CANCER

In every age, there is a word associated with a disease or plague that causes humans to shudder. In the 21st century, that word is "cancer." Just as cancer is the leading cause of death in humans, it claims nearly half the lives of dogs that die from a natural disease as well as half the dogs that die over the age of ten years.

Described as a genetic disease, cancer becomes a greater risk as the dog ages. Vets and dog owners have become increasingly aware of the threat of cancer to dogs. Statistics reveal that one dog in every five will develop cancer, the most common of which is skin cancer. Many cancers, including prostate, ovarian and breast cancer, can be avoided by spaying and neutering our dogs by the age of six months.

Early detection of cancer can save or extend a dog's life, so it is absolutely vital for owners to have their dogs examined by a qualified vet or oncologist immediately upon detection of any abnormality. Certain dietary guidelines have also proven to reduce the onset and spread of cancer. Foods based on fish rather than beef, due to the presence of Omega-3 fatty acids, are recommended. Other amino acids such as glutamine have significant benefits for canines, particularly those breeds that show a greater susceptibility to cancer.

Cancer management and treatments promise hope for future generations of canines. Since the disease is genetic, breeders should never breed a dog whose parents, grandparents and any related siblings have developed cancer. It is difficult to know whether to exclude an otherwise healthy dog from a breeding program, as the disease does not manifest itself until the dog's senior years.

RECOGNIZE CANCER WARNING SIGNS

Since early detection can possibly rescue your dog from becoming a cancer statistic, it is essential for owners to recognize the possible signs and seek the assistance of a qualified professional.

- Abnormal bumps or lumps that continue to grow
- Bleeding or discharge from any body cavity
- Persistent stiffness or lameness
- Recurrent sores or sores that do not heal
- Inappetence
- Breathing difficulties
- Weight loss
- Bad breath or odors
- General malaise and fatigue
- Eating and swallowing problems
- Difficulty urinating and defecating

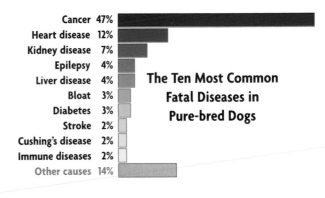

Disease	%
Cancer	47%
Heart disease	12%
Kidney disease	7%
Epilepsy	4%
Liver disease	4%
Bloat	3%
Diabetes	3%
Stroke	2%
Cushing's disease	2%
Immune diseases	2%
Other causes	14%

The Ten Most Common Fatal Diseases in Pure-bred Dogs

VITAL SIGNS

A dog's normal temperature is 101.5 degrees Fahrenheit. A range of between 100.0 and 102.5 degrees should be considered normal, as each dog's body sets its own temperature. It will be helpful if you take your dog's temperature when you know he is healthy and record it. Then, when you suspect that he is not feeling well, you will have a normal figure to compare the abnormal temperature against.

The normal pulse rate for a dog is between 100 and 125 beats per minute.

exams are necessary for all Cotons; while some hereditary problems are evident at birth, others do not present themselves until later in a dog's life.

There are a number of eye problems that have been documented in the Coton de Tuléar breed as being hereditary in nature, some more serious than others. All should be taken seriously, and affected dogs should never be used for breeding.

A cataract refers to opacity (cloudiness) of the eye's lens. A dog may develop a cataract in one or both eyes, and the severity of the cataract varies, as does the area of the eye that it covers. Surgery to remove the cataract is a common procedure that is likely to be successful. Cataracts can

develop as results of other diseases or of injuries, but they are also passed through heredity.

Retinal dysplasia (RD) is a malformation of the retina, which is the membrane responsible for receiving light, which then travels to the optic nerve to be transmitted to the brain, resulting in the images that are seen. When the retina does not develop properly, several problems can result. In slight cases, the dog's vision may not be affected at all. In more serious cases, the dog will have "spots" in his field of vision, meaning that part of the image is blocked out. In the worst case, the dog will be rendered completely blind.

In some dogs, the openings of the tear ducts may be very narrow or not present at all, causing tears to run over onto the dog's face. This sometimes can be corrected surgically.

Distichiasis refers to extra eyelashes or abnormally placed eyelashes. Sometimes these lashes grow in the inner eyelids and can irritate the cornea and the conjunctiva. Treatment to remove these lashes is available.

Persistent pupillary membrane (PPM) occurs when thin blood vessels around the eye, which are supposed to disappear by six weeks of age, remain. They can cause opacity if they adhere to the cornea or lens. Currently no treatment for PPM exists.

CDS: COGNITIVE DYSFUNCTION SYNDROME
"OLD-DOG SYNDROME"

There are many ways to evaluate old-dog syndrome. Veterinarians have defined CDS (cognitive dysfunction syndrome) as the gradual deterioration of cognitive abilities. These are indicated by changes in the dog's behavior. When a dog changes his routine response, and maladies have been eliminated as the cause of these behavioral changes, then CDS is the usual diagnosis.

More than half the dogs over eight years old suffer from some form of CDS. The older the dog, the more chance he has of suffering from CDS. In humans, doctors often dismiss the CDS behavioral changes as part of "winding down."

There are four major signs of CDS: the dog has frequent potty accidents inside the home, sleeps much more or much less than normal, acts confused and fails to respond to social stimuli.

SYMPTOMS OF CDS

FREQUENT POTTY ACCIDENTS
- *Urinates in the house.*
- *Defecates in the house.*
- *Doesn't signal that he wants to go out.*

SLEEP PATTERNS
- *Moves much more slowly.*
- *Sleeps more than normal during the day.*
- *Sleeps less during the night.*

CONFUSION
- *Goes outside and just stands there.*
- *Appears confused with a faraway look in his eyes.*
- *Hides more often.*
- *Doesn't recognize friends.*
- *Doesn't come when called.*
- *Walks around listlessly and without a destination.*

FAILURE TO RESPOND TO SOCIAL STIMULI
- *Comes to people less frequently, whether called or not.*
- *Doesn't tolerate petting for more than a short time.*
- *Doesn't come to the door when you return home.*

A male dog flea, *Ctenocephalides canis*.

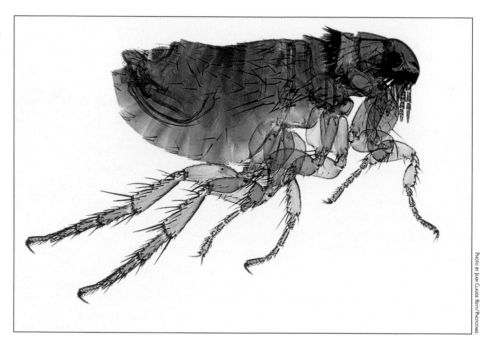

PHOTO BY JEAN CLAUDE REVY/PHOTOTAKE.

EXTERNAL PARASITES

FLEAS

Of all the problems to which dogs are prone, none is more well known and frustrating than fleas. Flea infestation is relatively simple to cure but difficult to prevent. Parasites that are harbored inside the body are a bit more difficult to eradicate but they are easier to control.

To control flea infestation, you have to understand the flea's life cycle. Fleas are often thought of as a summertime problem, but centrally heated homes have changed the patterns and fleas can be found at any time of the year. The most effective method of flea control is a two-stage approach: one stage to kill the adult fleas, and the other to control the development of pre-adult fleas. Unfortunately, no single active ingredient is effective against all stages of the life cycle.

FLEA KILLER CAUTION— "POISON"

Flea-killers are poisonous. You should not spray these toxic chemicals on areas of a dog's body that he licks, including his genitals and his face. Flea killers taken internally are a better answer, but check with your vet in case internal therapy is not advised for your dog.

LIFE CYCLE STAGES

During its life, a flea will pass through four life stages: egg, larva, pupa or nymph and adult. The adult stage is the most visible and irritating stage of the flea life cycle, and this is why the majority of flea-control products concentrate on this stage. The fact is that adult fleas account for only 1% of the total flea population, and the other 99% exist in pre-adult stages, i.e., eggs, larvae and nymphs. The pre-adult stages are barely visible to the naked eye.

THE LIFE CYCLE OF THE FLEA

Eggs are laid on the dog, usually in quantities of about 20 or 30, several times a day. The adult female flea must have a blood meal before each egg-laying session. When first laid, the eggs will cling to the dog's hair, as the eggs are still moist. However, they will quickly dry out and fall from the dog, especially if the dog moves around or scratches. Many eggs will fall off in the dog's favorite area or an area in which he spends a lot of time, such as his bed.

Once the eggs fall from the dog onto the carpet or furniture, they will hatch into larvae. This takes from one to ten days. Larvae are not particularly mobile and will usually travel only a few inches from where they hatch. However, they do have a tendency to move away from bright light and heavy

EN GARDE:
CATCHING FLEAS OFF GUARD!
Consider the following ways to arm yourself against fleas:
- Add a small amount of pennyroyal or eucalyptus oil to your dog's bath. These natural remedies repel fleas.
- Supplement your dog's food with fresh garlic (minced or grated) and a hearty amount of brewer's yeast, both of which ward off fleas.
- Use a flea comb on your dog daily. Submerge fleas in a cup of bleach to kill them quickly.
- Confine the dog to only a few rooms to limit the spread of fleas in the home.
- Vacuum daily...and get all of the crevices! Dispose of the bag every few days until the problem is under control.
- Wash your dog's bedding daily. Cover cushions where your dog sleeps with towels, and wash the towels often.

traffic—under furniture and behind doors are common places to find high quantities of flea larvae.

The flea larvae feed on dead organic matter, including adult flea feces, until they are ready to change into adult fleas. Fleas will usually remain as larvae for around seven days. After this period, the larvae will pupate into protective pupae. While inside the pupae, the larvae will undergo metamorphosis and change into adult fleas. This can take as little time as a few days, but the adult fleas can remain inside the pupae waiting to hatch for up to two years. The pupae are signaled to hatch by certain stimuli, such as physical pressure—the pupae's being stepped on, heat from an animal's lying on the pupae or increased carbon-dioxide levels and vibrations—indicating that a suitable host is available.

Once hatched, the adult flea must feed within a few days. Once the adult flea finds a host, it will not leave voluntarily. It only becomes dislodged by grooming or the host animal's scratching. The adult flea will remain on the

PHOTO BY DWIGHT R. KUHN.

host for the duration of its life unless forcibly removed.

TREATING THE ENVIRONMENT AND THE DOG

Treating fleas should be a two-pronged attack. First, the environment needs to be treated; this includes carpets and furniture, especially the dog's bedding and areas underneath furniture. The environment should be treated with a household spray containing an Insect Growth Regulator (IGR) and an insecticide to kill the adult fleas. Most IGRs are effective against eggs and larvae; they actually mimic the fleas' own hormones and stop the eggs and larvae from developing into adult fleas. There are currently no treatments available to attack the pupa stage of the life cycle, so the adult insecticide is used to kill the newly hatched adult fleas before they find a host. Most IGRs are active for many months, while adult insecticides are only active

A scanning electron micrograph of a dog or cat flea, *Ctenocephalides*, magnified more than 100x. This image has been colorized for effect.

S. E. M. BY DR DENNIS KUNKEL, UNIVERSITY OF HAWAII.

THE LIFE CYCLE OF THE FLEA

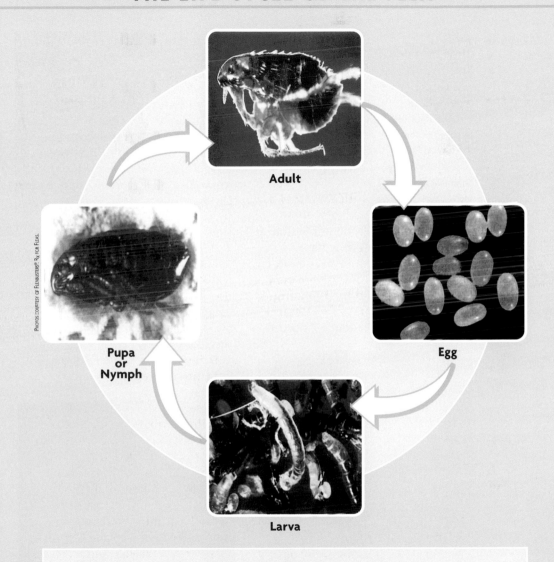

Adult

Egg

Larva

Pupa or Nymph

PHOTOS COURTESY OF FLEABUSTERS® Rx FOR FLEAS.

Fleas have been around for millions of years and have adapted to changing host animals. They are able to go through a complete life cycle in less than one month or they can extend their lives to almost two years by remaining as pupae or cocoons. They do not need blood or any other food for up to 20 months.

INSECT GROWTH REGULATOR (IGR)

Two types of products should be used when treating fleas—a product to treat the pet and a product to treat the home. Adult fleas represent less than 1% of the flea population. The pre-adult fleas (eggs, larvae and pupae) represent more than 99% of the flea population and are found in the environment; it is in the case of pre-adult fleas that products containing an Insect Growth Regulator (IGR) should be used in the home.

IGRs are a new class of compounds used to prevent the development of insects. They do not kill the insect outright, but instead use the insect's biology against it to stop it from completing its growth. Products that contain methoprene are the world's first and leading IGRs. Used to control fleas and other insects, this type of IGR will stop flea larvae from developing and protect the house for up to seven months.

The American dog tick, *Dermacentor variabilis*, is probably the most common tick found on dogs. Look at the strength in its eight legs! No wonder it's hard to detach them.

is to apply an adult insecticide to the dog. Traditionally, this would be in the form of a collar or a spray, but more recent innovations include digestible insecticides that poison the fleas when they ingest the dog's blood. Alternatively, there are drops that, when placed on the back of the dog's neck, spread throughout the hair and skin to kill adult fleas.

TICKS

Though not as common as fleas, ticks are found all over the tropical and temperate world. They don't bite, like fleas; they harpoon. They dig their sharp proboscis (nose) into the dog's skin and drink the blood. Their only food and drink is dog's

for a few days.

When treating with a household spray, it is a good idea to vacuum before applying the product. This stimulates as many pupae as possible to hatch into adult fleas. The vacuum cleaner should also be treated with an insecticide to prevent the eggs and larvae that have been collected in the vacuum bag from hatching.

The second stage of treatment

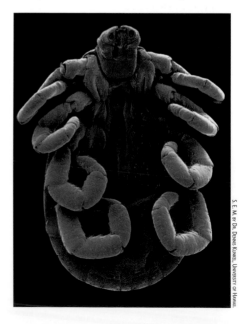

S. E. M. BY DR. DENNIS KUNKEL, UNIVERSITY OF HAWAII

blood. Dogs can get Lyme disease, Rocky Mountain spotted fever, tick bite paralysis and many other diseases from ticks. They may live where fleas are found and they like to hide in cracks or seams in walls. They are controlled the same way fleas are controlled.

The American dog tick, *Dermacentor variabilis*, may well be the most common dog tick in many geographical areas, especially those areas where the climate is hot and humid. Most dog ticks have life expectancies of a week to six months, depending upon climatic conditions. They can neither jump nor fly, but they can crawl slowly and can range up to 16 feet to reach a sleeping or unsuspecting dog.

MITES

Just as fleas and ticks can be problematic for your dog, mites can also lead to an itchy nuisance. Microscopic in size, mites are related to ticks and generally take up permanent residence on their host animal— in this case, your dog! The term *mange* refers to any infestation caused by one of the mighty mites, of which there are six varieties that concern dog owners.

Demodex mites cause a condition known as demodicosis (sometimes called red mange or

DEER-TICK CROSSING

The great outdoors may be fun for your dog, but it also is a home to dangerous ticks. Deer ticks carry a bacterium known as *Borrelia burgdorferi* and are most active in the autumn and spring. When infections are caught early, penicillin and tetracycline are effective antibiotics, but, if left untreated, the bacteria may cause neurological, kidney and cardiac problems as well as long-term trouble with walking and painful joints.

S. E. M. BY DR. ANDREW SPIELMAN/PHOTOTAKE.

PHOTO BY DR. DENNIS KUNKEL, UNIVERSITY OF HAWAII.

The head of an American dog tick, *Dermacentor variabilis*, enlarged and colorized for effect.

PHOTO BY JAMES HAYDEN/YOAV/PHOTOTAKE.

follicular mange), in which the mites live in the dog's hair follicles and sebaceous glands in larger-than-normal numbers.

This type of mange is commonly passed from the dam to her puppies and usually shows up on the puppies' muzzles, though demodicosis is not transferable from one normal dog to another. Most dogs recover from this type of mange without any treatment, though topical therapies are commonly prescribed by the vet.

The *Cheyletiellosis* mite is the hook-mouthed culprit associated

Human lice look like dog lice; the two are closely related.
PHOTO BY DWIGHT R. KUHN.

with "walking dandruff," a condition that affects dogs as well as cats and rabbits. This mite lives on the surface of the animal's skin and is readily transferable through direct or indirect contact with an affected animal. The dandruff is present in the form of scaly skin, which may or may not be itchy. If not treated, this mange can affect a whole kennel of dogs and can be spread to humans as well.

The *Sarcoptes* mite causes intense itching on the dog in the form of a condition known as scabies or sarcoptic mange. The cycle of the *Sarcoptes* mite lasts about three weeks, and the mites live in the top layer of the dog's skin (epidermis), preferably in areas with little hair. Scabies is highly contagious and can be passed to humans. Sometimes an allergic reaction to the mite worsens the severe itching associated with sarcoptic mange.

Ear mites, *Otodectes cynotis,* lead to otodectic mange, which most commonly affects the outer ear canal of the dog, though other areas can be affected as well. Dogs with ear-mite infestation commonly scratch at their ears, causing further irritation, and shake their heads. Dark brown droppings in the outer ear confirm the diagnosis. Your vet can prescribe a treatment to flush out the ears and kill any eggs in the ears. A complete month of treatment is necessary to cure the mange.

Two other mites, less common in dogs, include *Dermanyssus gallinae* (the poultry or red mite) and *Eutrombicula alfreddugesi* (the North American mite associated with trombiculidiasis or chigger infestation). The poultry mite frequently lives on chickens, but can transfer to dogs who spend time near farm animals. Chigger infestation affects dogs in the

---

NOT A DROP TO DRINK
Never allow your dog to swim in polluted water or public areas where water quality can be suspect. Even perfectly clear water can harbor parasites, many of which can cause serious to fatal illnesses in canines. Areas inhabited by water-fowl and other wildlife are especially dangerous.

Central US who have exposure to woodlands. The types of mange caused by both of these mites are treatable by vets.

INTERNAL PARASITES
Most animals—fishes, birds and mammals, including dogs and humans—have worms and other parasites that live inside their bodies. According to Dr. Herbert R. Axelrod, the fish pathologist, there are two kinds of parasites: dumb and smart. The smart parasites live in peaceful cooperation with their hosts (symbiosis), while the dumb parasites kill their hosts. Most worm infections are relatively easy to control. If they are not controlled, they weaken the host dog to the point that other medical problems occur, but they do not kill the host as dumb parasites would.

A brown dog tick, *Rhipicephalus sanguineus,* is an uncommon but annoying tick found on dogs.

DO NOT MIX
Never mix parasite-control products without first consulting your vet. Some products can become toxic when combined with others and can cause fatal consequences.

PHOTO BY CAROLINA BIOLOGICAL SUPPLY/PHOTOTAKE.

The roundworm *Rhabditis* can infect both dogs and humans.

ROUNDWORMS

Average-size dogs can pass 1,360,000 roundworm eggs every day. For example, if there were only 1 million dogs in the world, the world would be saturated with thousands of tons of dog feces. These feces would contain around 15,000,000,000 roundworm eggs.

Up to 31% of home yards and children's sand boxes in the US contain roundworm eggs.

Flushing dog's feces down the toilet is not a safe practice because the usual sewage treatments do not destroy roundworm eggs.

Infected puppies start shedding roundworm eggs at three weeks of age. They can be infected by their mother's milk.

The roundworm, *Ascaris lumbricoides*.

PHOTO BY DWIGHT R. KUHN.

ROUNDWORMS

The roundworms that infect dogs are known scientifically as *Toxocara canis*. They live in the dog's intestines and shed eggs continually. It has been estimated that a dog produces about 6 or more ounces of feces every day. Each ounce of feces averages hundreds of thousands of roundworm eggs. There are no known areas in which dogs roam that do not contain roundworm eggs. The greatest danger of roundworms is that they infect people, too! It is wise to have your dog tested regularly for roundworms.

In young puppies, roundworms cause bloated bellies, diarrhea, coughing and vomiting, and are transmitted from the dam (through blood or milk). Affected puppies will not appear as animated as normal puppies. The worms appear spaghetti-like, measuring as long as 6 inches. Adult dogs can acquire roundworms through coprophagia (eating contaminated feces) or by killing rodents that carry roundworms.

Roundworm infection can kill puppies and cause severe problems in adults, as the hatched larvae travel to the lungs and trachea through the bloodstream. Cleanliness is the best preventative for roundworms. Always pick up after your dog and dispose of feces in appropriate receptacles.

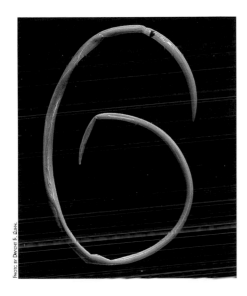

PHOTO BY DWIGHT R. KUHN.

HOOKWORMS

In the United States, dog owners have to be concerned about four different species of hookworm, the most common and most serious of which is *Ancylostoma caninum,* which prefers warm climates. The others are *Ancylostoma braziliense, Ancylostoma tubaeforme* and *Uncinaria stenocephala,* the latter of which is a concern to dogs living in the Northern US and Canada, as this species prefers cold climates. Hookworms are dangerous to humans as well as to dogs and cats, and can be the cause of severe anemia due to iron deficiency. The worm uses its teeth to attach itself to the dog's intestines and changes the site of its attachment about six times per day. Each time the worm

repositions itself, the dog loses blood and can become anemic. *Ancylostoma caninum* is the most likely of the four species to cause anemia in the dog.

Symptoms of hookworm infection include dark stools, weight loss, general weakness, pale coloration and anemia, as well as possible skin problems. Fortunately, hookworms are easily purged from the affected dog with a number of medications that have proven effective. Discuss these with your vet. Most heartworm preventatives include a hookworm insecticide as well.

Owners also must be aware that hookworms can infect humans, who can acquire the larvae through exposure to contaminated feces. Since the worms cannot complete their life cycle on a human, the worms simply infest the skin and cause irritation. This condition is known as cutaneous larva migrans syndrome. As a preventative, use disposable gloves or a "poop-scoop" to pick up your dog's droppings and prevent your dog (or neighborhood cats) from defecating in children's play areas.

The hookworm, *Ancylostoma caninum.*

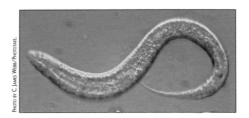

PHOTO BY C. JAMES WEBB/PHOTOTAKE.

The infective stage of the hookworm larva.

TAPEWORMS

Humans, rats, squirrels, foxes, coyotes, wolves and domestic dogs are all susceptible to tapeworm infection. Except in humans, tapeworms are usually not a fatal infection. Infected individuals can harbor 1000 parasitic worms.

Tapeworms, like some other types of worm, are hermaphroditic, meaning male and female in the same worm.

If dogs eat infected rats or mice, or anything else infected with tapeworm, they get the tapeworm disease. One month after attaching to a dog's intestine, the worm starts shedding eggs. These eggs are infective immediately. Infective eggs can live for a few months without a host animal.

The head and rostellum (the round prominence on the scolex) of a tapeworm, which infects dogs and humans.

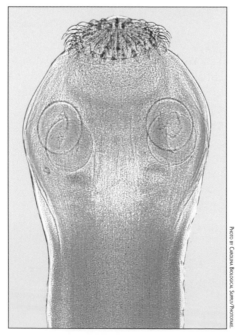

PHOTO BY CAROLINA BIOLOGICAL SUPPLY/PHOTOTAKE.

TAPEWORMS

There are many species of tapeworm, all of which are carried by fleas! The most common tapeworm affecting dogs is known as *Dipylidium caninum*. The dog eats the flea and starts the tapeworm cycle. Humans can also be infected with tapeworms—so don't eat fleas! Fleas are so small that your dog could pass them onto your hands, your plate or your food and thus make it possible for you to ingest a flea that is carrying tapeworm eggs.

While tapeworm infection is not life-threatening in dogs (smart parasite!), it can be the cause of a very serious liver disease for humans. About 50% of the humans infected with *Echinococcus multilocularis*, a type of tapeworm that causes alveolar hydatid, perish.

WHIPWORMS

In North America, whipworms are counted among the most common parasitic worms in dogs. The whipworm's scientific name is *Trichuris vulpis*. These worms attach themselves in the lower parts of the intestine, where they feed. Affected dogs may only experience upset tummies, colic and diarrhea. These worms, however, can live for months or years in the dog, beginning their larval stage in the small intestine, spending their adult stage in the large intestine and finally passing infective eggs through the dog's feces. The only way to detect whipworms is through a fecal examination, though this is not always foolproof. Treatment for whipworms is tricky, due to the worms' unusual life-cycle pattern, and very often dogs are reinfected due to exposure to infective eggs on the ground. The whipworm eggs can survive in the environment for as long as five years; thus, cleaning up droppings in your own backyard as well as in public places is absolutely essential for sanitation purposes and the health of your dog and others.

THREADWORMS
Though less common than round-worms, hookworms and those previously mentioned, thread-worms concern dog owners in the Southwestern US and Gulf Coast area where the climate is hot and humid. Living in the small intestine of the dog, this worm measures a mere 2 millimeters and is round in shape. Like that of the whipworm, the threadworm's life cycle is very complex and the eggs and larvae are passed through the feces. A deadly disease in humans, *Strongyloides* readily infects people, and the handling of feces is the most common means of transmission. Threadworms are most often seen in young puppies; bloody diarrhea and pneumonia are symptoms. Sick puppies must be isolated and treated immediately; vets recommend a follow-up treatment one month later.

HEARTWORM PREVENTATIVES

There are many heartworm preventatives on the market, many of which are sold at your veterinarian's office. These products can be given daily or monthly, depending on the manufacturer's instructions. All of these preventatives contain chemical insecticides directed at killing heartworms, which leads to some controversy among dog owners. In effect, heartworm preventatives are necessary evils, though you should determine how necessary based on your pet's lifestyle. There is no doubt that heartworm is a dreadful disease that threatens the lives of dogs. However, the likelihood of your dog's being bitten by an infected mosquito is slim in most places, and a mosquito-repellent (or an herbal remedy such as Wormwood or Black Walnut) is much safer for your dog and will not compromise his immune system (the way heartworm preventatives will). Should you decide to use the traditional preventative "medications," you can consider giving the pill every other or third month. Since the toxins in the pill will kill the heartworms at all stages of development, the pill would be effective in killing larvae, nymphs or adults, and it takes four months for the larvae to reach the adult stage. Thus, there is no rationale to poisoning the dog's system on a monthly basis. Lastly, do not give the pill during the winter months, since there are no mosquitoes around to pass on their infection, unless you live in a tropical environment.

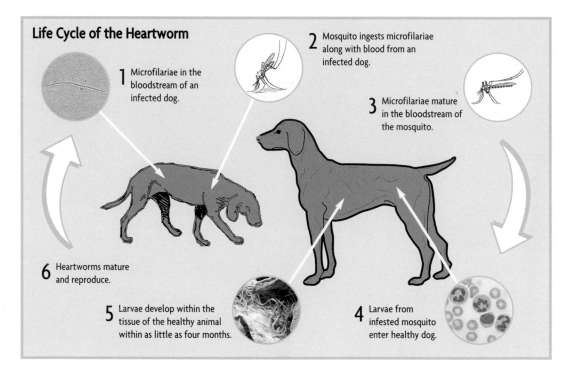

Life Cycle of the Heartworm

1 Microfilariae in the bloodstream of an infected dog.

2 Mosquito ingests microfilariae along with blood from an infected dog.

3 Microfilariae mature in the bloodstream of the mosquito.

6 Heartworms mature and reproduce.

5 Larvae develop within the tissue of the healthy animal within as little as four months.

4 Larvae from infested mosquito enter healthy dog.

HEARTWORMS

Heartworms are thin, extended worms up to 12 inches long, which live in a dog's heart and the major blood vessels surrounding it. Dogs may have up to 200 worms. Symptoms may be loss of energy, loss of appetite, coughing, the development of a pot belly and anemia.

Heartworms are transmitted by mosquitoes. The mosquito drinks the blood of an infected dog and takes in larvae with the blood. The larvae, called microfilariae, develop within the body of the mosquito and are passed on to the next dog bitten after the larvae mature. It takes two to three weeks for the larvae to develop to the infective stage within the body of the mosquito. Dogs are usually treated at about six weeks of age and maintained on a prophylactic dose given monthly.

Blood testing for heartworms is not necessarily indicative of how seriously your dog is infected. Although this is a dangerous disease, it is not easy for a dog to be infected. Discuss the various preventatives with your vet, as there are many different types now available. Together you can decide on a safe course of prevention for your dog.

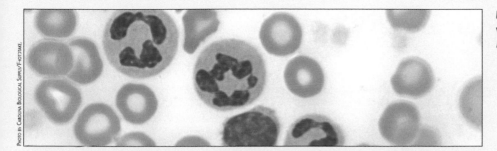

Magnified heart-worm larvae, *Dirofilaria immitis.*

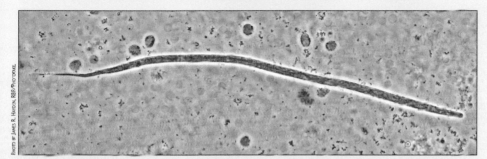

Heartworm, *Dirofilaria immitis.*

The heart of a dog infected with canine heart-worm, *Dirofilaria immitis.*

HOMEOPATHY:
an alternative
to conventional
medicine

"Less is Most"

Using this principle, the strength of a homeopathic remedy is measured by the number of serial dilutions that were undertaken to create it. The greater the number of serial dilutions, the greater the strength of the homeopathic remedy. The potency of a remedy that has been made by making a dilution of 1 part in 100 parts (or 1/100) is 1c or 1cH. If this remedy is subjected to a series of further dilutions, each one being 1/100, a more dilute and stronger remedy is produced. If the remedy is diluted in this way six times, it is called 6c or 6cH. A dilution of 6c is 1 part in 1,000,000,000,000. In general, higher potencies in more frequent doses are better for acute symptoms and lower potencies in more infrequent doses are more useful for chronic, long-standing problems.

CURING OUR DOGS NATURALLY

Holistic medicine means treating the whole animal as a unique, perfect, living being. Generally, holistic treatments do not suppress the symptoms that the body naturally produces, as do most medications prescribed by conventional doctors and vets. Holistic methods seek to cure disease by regaining balance and harmony in the patient's environment. Some of these methods include use of nutritional therapy, herbs, flower essences, aromatherapy, acupuncture, massage, chiropractic and, of course, the most popular holistic approach, homeopathy.

Homeopathy is a theory or system of treating illness with small doses of substances which, if administered in larger quantities, would produce the symptoms that the patient already has. This approach is often described as "like cures like." Although modern veterinary medicine is geared toward the "quick fix," homeopathy relies on the belief that, given the time, the body is able to heal itself and return to its natural, healthy state.

Choosing a remedy to cure a problem in our dogs is the difficult part of homeopathy. Consult with your vet for a professional diagnosis of your dog's symptoms. Often

these symptoms require immediate conventional care. If your vet is willing and knowledgeable, you may attempt a homeopathic remedy. Be aware that cortisone prevents homeopathic remedies from working. There are hundreds of possibilities and combinations to cure many problems in dogs, from basic physical problems such as excessive shedding, fleas or other parasites, unattractive doggy odor, bad breath, upset tummy, obesity, dry, oily or dull coat, diarrhea, ear problems or eye discharge (including tears and dry or mucousy matter), to behavioral abnormalities such as fear of loud noises, habitual licking, disinterest in food, excessive barking and various phobias. From alumina to zincum metallicum, the remedies span the planet and the imagination,,,from flowers and weeds to chemicals, insect droppings, diesel smoke and volcanic ash.

Using "Like to Treat Like"

Unlike conventional medicines that suppress symptoms, homeopathic remedies treat illnesses with small doses of substances that, if administered in larger quantities, would produce the symptoms that the patient already has. While the same homeopathic remedy can be used to treat different symptoms in different dogs, here are some interesting remedies and their uses.

Apis Mellifica
(made from honey bee venom) can be used for allergies or to reduce swelling that occurs in acutely infected kidneys.

Diesel Smoke
can be used to help control travel sickness.

Calcarea Fluorica
(made from calcium fluoride, which helps harden bone structure) can be useful in treating hard lumps in tissues.

Natrum Muriaticum
(made from common salt, sodium chloride) is useful in treating thin, thirsty dogs.

Nitricum Acidum
(made from nitric acid) is used for symptoms you would expect to see from contact with acids, such as lesions, especially where the skin joins the linings of body orifices or openings such as the lips and nostrils.

Symphytum
(made from the herb Knitbone, *Symphytum officinale*) is used to encourage bones to heal.

Urtica Urens
(made from the common stinging nettle) is used in treating painful, irritating rashes.

HOMEOPATHIC REMEDIES FOR YOUR DOG

Symptom/Ailment	Possible Remedy
ALLERGIES	Apis Mellifica 30c, Astacus Fluviatilis 6c, Pulsatilla 30c, Urtica Urens 6c
ALOPECIA	Alumina 30c, Lycopodium 30c, Sepia 30c, Thallium 6c
ANAL GLANDS (BLOCKED)	Hepar Sulphuris Calcareum 30c, Sanicula 6c, Silicea 6c
ARTHRITIS	Rhus Toxicodendron 6c, Bryonia Alba 6c
CATARACT	Calcarea Carbonica 6c, Conium Maculatum 6c, Phosphorus 30c, Silicea 30c
CONSTIPATION	Alumina 6c, Carbo Vegetabilis 30c, Graphites 6c, Nitricum Acidum 30c, Silicea 6c
COUGHING	Aconitum Napellus 6c, Belladonna 30c, Hyoscyamus Niger 30c, Phosphorus 30c
DIARRHEA	Arsenicum Album 30c, Aconitum Napellus 6c, Chamomilla 30c, Mercurius Corrosivus 30c
DRY EYE	Zincum Metallicum 30c
EAR PROBLEMS	Aconitum Napellus 30c, Belladonna 30c, Hepar Sulphuris 30c, Tellurium 30c, Psorinum 200c
EYE PROBLEMS	Borax 6c, Aconitum Napellus 30c, Graphites 6c, Staphysagria 6c, Thuja Occidentalis 30c
GLAUCOMA	Aconitum Napellus 30c, Apis Mellifica 6c, Phosphorus 30c
HEAT STROKE	Belladonna 30c, Gelsemium Sempervirens 30c, Sulphur 30c
HICCOUGHS	Cinchona Deficinalis 6c
HIP DYSPLASIA	Colocynthis 6c, Rhus Toxicodendron 6c, Bryonia Alba 6c
INCONTINENCE	Argentum Nitricum 6c, Causticum 30c, Conium Maculatum 30c, Pulsatilla 30c, Sepia 30c
INSECT BITES	Apis Mellifica 30c, Cantharis 30c, Hypericum Perforatum 6c, Urtica Urens 30c
ITCHING	Alumina 30c, Arsenicum Album 30c, Carbo Vegetabilis 30c, Hypericum Perforatum 6c, Mezerium 6c, Sulphur 30c
KENNEL COUGH	Drosera 6c, Ipecacuanha 30c
MASTITIS	Apis Mellifica 30c, Belladonna 30c, Urtica Urens 1m
MOTION SICKNESS	Cocculus 6c, Petroleum 6c
PATELLAR LUXATION	Gelsemium Sempervirens 6c, Rhus Toxicodendron 6c
PENIS PROBLEMS	Aconitum Napellus 30c, Hepar Sulphuris Calcareum 30c, Pulsatilla 30c, Thuja Occidentalis 6c
PUPPY TEETHING	Calcarea Carbonica 6c, Chamomilla 6c, Phytolacca 6c

Recognizing a Sick Dog

Unlike colicky babies and cranky children, our canine kids cannot tell us when they are feeling ill. Therefore, there are a number of signs that owners can identify to know that their dogs are not feeling well.

Take note for physical manifestations such as:

- unusual, bad odor, including bad breath
- excessive shedding
- wax in the ears, chronic ear irritation
- oily, flaky, dull haircoat
- mucus, tearing or similar discharge in the eyes
- fleas or mites
- mucus in stool, diarrhea
- sensitivity to petting or handling
- licking at paws, scratching face, etc.

Keep an eye out for behavioral changes as well including:

- lethargy, idleness
- lack of patience or general irritability
- lack of appetite
- phobias (fear of people, loud noises, etc.)
- strange behavior, suspicion, fear
- coprophagia
- more frequent barking
- whimpering, crying

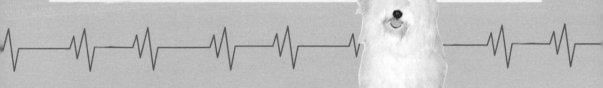

Get Well Soon

You don't need a DVM to provide good TLC to your sick or recovering dog, but you do need to pay attention to some details that normally wouldn't bother him. The following tips will aid Fido's recovery and get him back on his paws again:

- Keep his space free of irritating smells, like heavy perfumes and air fresheners.
- Rest is the best medicine! Avoid harsh lighting that will prevent your dog from sleeping. Shade him from bright sunlight during the day and dim the lights in the evening.
- Keep the noise level down. Animals are more sensitive to sound when they are sick.

- Be attentive to any necessary temperature adjustments. A dog with a fever needs a cool room and cold liquids. A bitch that is whelping or recovering from surgery will be more comfortable in a warm room, consuming warm liquids and food.
- You wouldn't send a sick child back to school early, so don't rush your dog back into a full routine until he seems absolutely ready.

COTON DE TULÉAR

As a Coton owner, you have selected your dog so that you and your loved ones can have a companion, a clown, a friend and a four-legged family member. You invest time, money and effort to care for and train the family's new charge. Of course, this chosen canine behaves perfectly! Well, perfectly like a *dog*.

THINK LIKE A DOG

Dogs do not think like humans, nor do humans think like dogs, though we try. Unfortunately, a dog is incapable of comprehending how humans think, so the responsibility falls on the owner to adopt a viable canine mindset. Dogs cannot rationalize, and they exist in the present moment. Many a dog owner makes the mistake in training of thinking that he can reprimand his dog for something that the dog did a while ago. Basically, you cannot even reprimand a dog for something he did 20 seconds ago! Either catch him in the act or forget it! It is a waste of your and your dog's time—in his mind, you are reprimanding him for whatever he is doing at that moment.

The following behavioral problems represent some which owners most commonly encounter. Every dog is unique and every situation is unique. No author could purport for you to solve your Coton's problems simply by reading a chapter in a breed book. Here we outline some basic "dogspeak" so that owners' chances of solving behavioral problems are increased. Discuss bad habits with your vet and he can recommend a behavioral specialist to consult in appropriate cases. Since behavioral abnormalities are the main reason for owners' abandoning their pets, we hope that you will make a valiant effort to solve your Coton's problems. Patience and understanding are virtues that must dwell in every pet-loving household.

SEPARATION ANXIETY

Recognized by behaviorists as the most common form of stress for dogs, separation anxiety can also lead to destructive behaviors in your dog. It's more than your Coton's howling his displeasure at your leaving the house and his being left alone. This is a normal reaction, no different than the child who cries as his mother leaves him on the first day at school. Separation anxiety is more serious. In fact, if you are constantly with your dog, he will come to expect you with him all of the time, making it even more traumatic for him when you are not there.

Obviously, you enjoy spending time with your dog, and he thrives on your love and attention. However, it should not become a dependent relationship in which he is heartbroken without you. This broken heart can also bring on destructive behavior as well as loss of appetite, depression and lack of interest in play and interaction. Canine behaviorists have been spending much time and energy to help owners better understand the significance of this stressful condition.

One thing you can do to minimize separation anxiety is to make your entrances and exits as low-key as possible. Do not give your dog a long drawn-out good-bye, and do not lavish him with hugs and kisses when you return. This is giving in to the attention that he craves, and it will only make him miss it more when you are away. Another thing you can try is to give your dog a treat when you leave; this will not only keep him occupied and keep his mind off the fact that you have just left, but it will also help him associate your leaving with a pleasant experience.

You may have to accustom your dog to being left alone in intervals. Of course, when your dog starts whimpering as you approach the door, your first

"LONELY WOLF"

The number of dogs that suffer from separation anxiety is on the rise as more and more pet owners find themselves at work all day. New attention is being paid to this problem, which is especially hard to diagnose since it is only evident when the dog is alone. Research is currently being done to help educate dog owners about separation anxiety and how they can help minimize this problem in their dogs.

instinct will be to run to him and comfort him, but do not do it! Eventually he will adjust to your absence. His anxiety stems from being placed in an unfamiliar situation; by familiarizing him with being alone, he will learn that he will survive. That is not to say you should purposely leave your dog home alone, but the dog needs to know that, while he can depend on you for his care, you do not have to be by his side 24 hours a day. Some behaviorists recommend tiring the dog out before you leave home—take him for a walk or engage in a game of fetch in the yard.

When the dog is alone in the house, he should be placed in his crate—another distinct advantage to crate-training your dog. The crate should be placed in his familiar happy family area, where he normally sleeps and already feels comfortable, thereby making him feel more at ease when he is alone. Be sure to give the dog a special chew toy to enjoy while he settles into his crate.

AGGRESSION

This is a problem that concerns all responsible dog owners, although an aggressive Coton is hard to find. However, it doesn't hurt to recognize the signs. An aggressive dog, no matter the size,

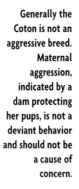

Generally the Coton is not an aggressive breed. Maternal aggression, indicated by a dam protecting her pups, is not a deviant behavior and should not be a cause of concern.

may lunge at, bite or even attack a person or another dog. Aggressive behavior is not to be tolerated. It is more than just inappropriate behavior; it is painful for a family to watch their dog become unpredictable in his behavior to the point where they are afraid of him. While not all aggressive behavior is dangerous, things like growling, baring teeth, etc., can be frightening. It is important to ascertain why the dog is acting in this manner. Aggression is a display of dominance, and the dog should not have the dominant role in his pack, which is, in this case, your family.

It is important not to challenge an aggressive dog. An aggressive dog's signals include making direct eye contact, staring and trying to make himself appear as large as possible: ears pricked, chest out, tail erect. Height and size signify authority in a dog pack—being taller or "above" another dog literally means that he is "above" in social status. These body signals tell you that a dog thinks he is in charge, a problem that needs to be addressed. An aggressive dog is unpredictable; you never know when he is going to strike and what he is going to do. You cannot understand why a dog that is playful one minute is growling the next.

Fear is a common cause of aggression in dogs. If your Coton exhibits any signs of aggression,

fear could be the reason. Perhaps your Coton had a negative experience as a puppy, which causes him to be fearful when a similar situation presents itself later in life. The dog may act aggressively in order to protect himself from whatever is making him afraid.

It is not always easy to determine what is making your dog fearful, but if you can isolate what brings out the fear reaction, you can help the dog get over it. Supervise your Coton's interactions with people and other dogs, and praise the dog when it goes well. If he starts to act aggressively in a situation, correct him and remove him from the situation. Do not let people approach the dog and start petting him without your express permission. That way, you can have the dog sit to accept petting, and praise him when he behaves properly. You are focusing on praise and on modifying his behavior by rewarding him when he acts appropriately. By being gentle and by

Getting to know you—dogs learn a lot by sniffing the rears of new friends.

supervising his interactions, you are showing him that there is no need to be afraid or defensive.

If you have problems with aggression in your Coton, the best solution is to consult a behavioral specialist, one who is familiar with the breed if possible. Together, perhaps you can pinpoint the cause of your dog's aggression and do something about it. If, very unusually, you find that your Coton has become aggressive, and therefore unpredictable in his behavior and untrustworthy, you may feel it necessary to seek a new home with a more suitable family and environment. If this is the case, you must explain fully to the new owners all of your reasons for rehoming the dog to be fair to all concerned.

SEXUAL BEHAVIOR

Dogs exhibit certain sexual behaviors that may have influenced your choice of male or female when you first purchased your Coton. To a certain extent, spaying/neutering will eliminate these behaviors, but if you are purchasing a dog that you wish to breed from, you should be aware of what you will have to deal with throughout the dog's life.

Female dogs usually have two estruses per year, with each season lasting about three weeks. These are the only times in which a female dog will mate, and she usually will not allow this until the second week of the cycle, although this varies from bitch to bitch. If not bred during the heat cycle, it is not uncommon for a bitch to experience a false pregnancy, in which her mammary glands swell and she exhibits maternal tendencies toward toys or other objects.

With male dogs, owners must be aware that whole dogs (dogs who are not neutered) have the natural inclination to mark their territory. Males mark their territory by spraying small amounts of urine as they lift their legs in a macho ritual. Marking can occur both outdoors in the yard and around the neighborhood as well as indoors on furniture legs, curtains and the sofa. Such behavior can be very frustrating for the owner; early training is strongly urged before the "urge" strikes your dog. Neutering the male at an appropriate early age can solve this problem before it becomes a habit.

Other problems associated with males are wandering and mounting. Both of these habits, of course, belong to the unneutered dog, whose sexual drive leads him away from home in search of the bitch in heat. Males will mount females in heat, as well as any other dog, male or female, that happens to catch their fancy. Other possible mounting partners include his owner, the furniture, guests to the home and strangers on the street. Discourage such behavior early on.

Owners must further recognize that mounting is not merely a sexual expression but also one of dominance, seen in males and females alike. Be consistent and be persistent, and you will find that you can "move mounters."

CHEWING

The national canine pastime is chewing! Every dog loves to sink his "canines" into a tasty bone, so it is important to provide your dog with appropriate chew toys so that he doesn't destroy your possessions or make a habit of gnawing on your hands and fingers. Dogs need to chew to massage their gums, to make their new teeth feel better and to exercise their jaws. This is a natural behavior that is deeply embedded in all things canine. Our role as owners is not to stop the dog's chewing, but rather to redirect it to positive, chew-worthy objects. Be an informed owner and purchase proper chew toys, like strong nylon bones, that will not splinter. Be sure that the objects are safe and durable, since your dog's safety is at risk. Again, the owner is responsible for ensuring a dog-proof environment.

The best answer is prevention; that is, put your shoes, handbags and other tasty objects in their proper places (out of the reach of

TUG-OF-WAR
You should never play tug-of-war games with your puppy. Such games create a struggle for "top dog" position and teach the puppy that it is okay to challenge you. It will also encourage your puppy's natural tendency to bite down hard and *win*.

the growing canine mouth). Direct your puppy to his toys whenever you see him "tasting" the furniture legs or the leg of your jeans. Make a loud noise to attract the pup's attention and immediately escort him to his chew toy and engage him with the toy for at least four minutes, praising and encouraging him all the while. An array of safe, interesting chew toys will keep your dog's mind and teeth occupied, and distracted from chewing on things he shouldn't.

Some trainers recommend deterrents, such as hot pepper, a bitter spice or a product designed for this purpose, to discourage the dog from chewing unwanted objects. Test these products to see which works best before investing in large quantities.

FOOD STEALING

Is your dog devising ways of stealing food from your coffee table or kitchen counter? If so, you must answer the following questions: Is your Coton a bit hungry, or is he "constantly famished" like many dogs seem to be? Face it, some dogs are more food-motivated than others. They are totally obsessed by the smell of food and can only think of their next meal. Food stealing is terrific fun and always yields a great reward—*food*, glorious food.

Your goal as an owner, therefore, is to be sensible about where food is placed in the home and to reprimand your dog whenever he is caught in the act of stealing. But remember, only reprimand your dog if you actually see him stealing, not later when the crime is discovered; that will be of no

> **TRAINING TIP**
> To encourage proper barking, you can teach your dog the command "Quiet." When someone comes to the door and the dog barks a few times, praise him. Talk to him soothingly and, when he stops barking, tell him "Quiet" and continue to praise him. In this sense, you are letting him bark his warning, which is an instinctive behavior, and then rewarding him for remaining quiet. You may initially use a treat along with praise.

use at all and will only serve to confuse him.

BARKING

Dogs cannot talk—oh, what they would say if they could! Instead, barking is a dog's way of "talking." It can be somewhat frustrating because it is not always easy to tell what a dog means by his bark—is he excited, happy, frightened or angry? Whatever it is that the dog is trying to say, he should not be punished for barking. It is only when the barking becomes excessive, and when the excessive barking becomes a bad habit, that the behavior needs to be modified.

Fortunately, Cotons are not as vocal as most other dogs; they are not known as "yappers" or otherwise noisy dogs. However, if your Coton becomes an excessive habitual barker, you should correct the problem early on. As your Coton

The Coton is not a yapper, like some other Bichon breeds that will remain nameless! This is a discriminate, bright breed that uses its bark with purpose.

grows up, you will be able to tell when his barking is purposeful and when it is for no reason. You will become able to distinguish your dog's different barks and their meanings. For example, the bark when someone comes to the door will be different from the bark when he is excited to see you. It is similar to a person's tone of voice, except that the dog has to rely totally on tone of voice because he does not have the benefit of using words. An incessant barker will be evident at an early age.

There are some things that encourage a dog to bark. For example, if your dog barks non-stop for a few minutes and you give him a treat to quiet him, he believes that you are rewarding him for barking. He will associate barking with getting a treat and will keep doing it until he is rewarded. On the other hand, if you give him a command such as "Quiet" and praise him after he has stopped barking for a few seconds, he will get the idea that being "quiet" is what you want him to do.

BEGGING

Just like food stealing, begging is a favorite pastime of hungry Cotons! It achieves that same lovely result—*food!* Dogs quickly learn that their owners keep the "good food" for ourselves, and that we humans do not dine on dry food alone. Begging is a conditioned response related to a specific stimulus, time and place. The sounds of the kitchen, cans and bottles opening, crinkling bags, the smell of food in preparation, etc., will excite the dog, and soon the paws will be in the air!

Here is the solution to stopping this behavior: Although it may be difficult to resist the Coton's clownish antics and comic performances in hopes of a treat, never give in to a beggar! You are rewarding the dog for sitting pretty, jumping up, whining and rubbing his nose into you by giving him food. By ignoring the dog, you will (eventually) force the behavior into extinction. Note that the behavior is likely to get worse before it disappears, so

---

SAY NO TO THE BEGGAR!
Proverb: "All our hearts are bleeding for the dog that died of overfeeding." It is admittedly difficult to keep your feelings in check when your clever little Coton wags his tail like crazy, looks at you with sparkling, loving eyes and paws with his little feet like a kitten. But giving in to his begging, however cute, means that you are compromising his health. Rewarding a dog for good behavior is a different story; use nutritious dog treats that have been manufactured for this purpose and are available from pet shops.

NO KISSES
We all love our dogs and our dogs love us. They show their love and affection by licking us. This is not a very sanitary practice, as dogs lick and sniff in some unsavory places. Kissing your dog on the mouth is strictly forbidden, as parasites can be transmitted in this manner.

greeting may be, the chances are that your visitors will not appreciate your dog's enthusiasm. The dog will not be able to distinguish upon whom he can jump and whom he cannot. Therefore, it is probably best to discourage this behavior entirely.

Pick a command such as "Off" (avoid using "Down" since you will use that for the dog to lie down) and tell him "Off" when he jumps up. Place him on the ground on all fours and have him sit, praising him the whole time. Always lavish him with praise and petting when he is in the sit position. In this way, you can give him a warm affectionate greeting, let him know that you are as pleased to see him as he is to see you and instill good manners at the same time!

DIGGING

Digging, which is seen as a destructive behavior to humans, is actually quite a natural behavior in dogs. Although terriers (the "earth dogs") are most associated with the digging, any dog's desire to dig can be irrepressible and most frustrating to his owners... and remember the terriers in your Coton's early ancestry! When digging occurs in your yard, it is actually a normal behavior redirected into something the dog can do in his everyday life. In the wild, a dog would be actively seeking food, making his own

be sure there are not any "softies" in the family who will give in to little "Oliver" every time he whimpers, "More, please."

JUMPING UP

Jumping up is a dog's friendly way of saying hello! Some dog owners do not mind when their dog jumps up. The problem arises when guests come to the house and the dog greets them in the same manner—whether they like it or not! However friendly the shelter, etc. He would be using his paws in a purposeful manner for his survival. Since you provide him with food and shelter, he has no need to use his paws for these purposes, and so the energy that he would be using may manifest itself in the form of little holes all over your yard and flower beds.

Perhaps your dog is digging as a reaction to boredom—it is somewhat similar to someone eating a whole bag of chips in front of the TV—because they are there and there is nothing better to do! Basically, the answer is to provide the dog with adequate play and exercise so that his mind and paws are occupied, and so that he feels as if he is doing something useful.

Of course, digging is easiest to control if it is stopped as soon as possible, but it is often hard to catch a dog in the act. If your dog is a compulsive digger and is not easily distracted by other activities, you can designate an area on your property where he is allowed to dig. If you catch him digging in an off-limits area of the yard, immediately take him to the approved area and praise him for digging there. Keep a close eye on him so that you can catch him in the act—that is the only way to make him understand what is permitted and what is not. If you take him to a hole he dug an hour ago and tell him "No," he will understand that you are not fond of holes, dirt or flowers. If you catch him while he is stifle-deep in your tulips, that is when he will get your message.

COPROPHAGIA

Feces eating is, to humans, one of the most disgusting behaviors that their dogs could engage in; yet, to dogs, it is perfectly normal. It is hard for us to understand why a dog would want to eat his own feces. He could be seeking certain nutrients that are missing from his diet, he could be just hungry or he could be attracted by the pleasing (to a dog) scent. To discourage this behavior, first make sure that the food you are feeding your dog is nutritionally complete and that he is getting enough food. If changes in his diet do not seem to work, and no medical cause can be found, you will have to modify the behavior through environmental control before it becomes a habit. The best way to prevent your dog from eating his stool is to make it unavailable—clean up after he eliminates and remove any stool from the yard. If it is not there, he cannot eat it.

Reprimanding for stool eating rarely impresses the dog. Vets recommend distracting the dog while he is in the act of stool eating. Coprophagia is seen most frequently in pups 6 to 12 months of age, and usually disappears around the dog's first birthday.

Activities 111-112
Adaptability 17
Adult
—diet 69
—health 121
—training 88
Age 90
Aggression 17, 63, 148
—fear 86
Agility trials 111
Aging 121
Air travel 82
Allergy
—airborne 123
—food 123
—parasite bite 122
America 14
American dog tick **132-133**
American Kennel Club 14
American Rare Breed
   Association 14, 26, 40
Anal glands 80
Ancylostoma caninum **137**
ARBA 14, 26, 40
Ascaris lumbricoides **136**
Attention 102
Auto-immune illness 123
Axelrod, Dr. Herbert R. 135
Bad habits 25
Barking 17, 152
Bathing 76
Bedding 50-51, 66, 93
Bedlington Terriers 12
Begging 25, 153
Behavior 25
Behavioral problems 146
Belgian Dog Club 18
Best of Breed 30
Bichon breeds 10
Bichon Frisé 10, **12**
Black 20
Boarding 84
Body language 149
Bolognese **10**, 13, **15**
Bones 53, 151
Booster immunizations 119
Boredom 155
Borrelia burgdorferi 133

Bowls 56
Breed clubs 30, 39
Breed standard 26
—FCI 30
Breeder 14, 26, 39-41, 43,
   46, 124
—finding a 45
—selecting a 39
Breeding 42
Brown 20
Brown dog tick **135**
CAC 27
CACIB 27
Canadian Kennel Club 26
Cancer 24
Canine cough 119, 121
Canine development
   schedule 90
Car travel 81
Cat 101
Cataracts 126
CDS 127
Ceriez, Micky 18
*Certificat d'Aptitude au
   Championnat* 27
—*International de Beauté*
   27
Chew toys 52, 65-66, 151
Chewing 57, 65-66, 95, 151
Chien Coton 10
Children 24
Chocolate 61
Climbing 25, 58
Coat 9-10, 18, 44, 73
Cognitive dysfunction
   syndrome 127
Collar 54, 101
Color 10, 12, 18, 76
Colostrum 68
Come 107
Commands 103-109
Competitive events 111
Control 94
Coprophagia 155
Coronavirus 121
Coton de Tuléar Club 17
Coton de Tuléar Club of
   America 14

Cotton Swab Dog 10
Crate 49, 52, 66, 81-82, 93-
   94
—training 52, 91, 94-99,
   148
Crocodiles 13
Crufts Dog Show 111
Crying 61, 65
Ctenocephalides **130**
Ctenocephalides canis **128**
De Flacourt, Etienne 18
Deer tick **133**
Dental care 79, 120
Dental health 79, 117, 122
Dermacentor variabilis
   132-133
Destructive behavior 73,
   95, 146, 151, 155
Diet 24, 67, 124, 153
—adult 69
—change in 70
—grain-based 67
—puppy 68
—senior 70, 121
Digging 58, 154
Dipylidium caninum 138
Dirofilaria immitis **141**
Discipline 95, 100
Distemper 119, 121
Distichiasis 126
Dog flea **128**
Dog of royalty 13, 20
Dog tick **133**
Dominance 21, 64, 149, 151
Down 104
Down/stay 106
Ear cleaning 79
Ear mites 135
Ear stains 80
*Echinococcus multilocu-
   laris* 138
Energy level 17
England 112
Estrus 150
European Champions
   Show 30
Exercise 17, 24, 71
Exportation 10

External parasites 128-135
Eyes 18
—care 80
—diseases 124
—problems 41
Family dog 18, 24
Family introduction to pup
   59
FCI 12, 20, 26, 31
Fear 63, 149
Feces eating 155
Fédération Cynologique
   Internationale 12, 20,
   26, 31
Feeding 67, 124, 153
Fence 58, 72
First night home 60
Flea **128**, 129, **130-131,** 132,
   138
—life cycle 129-130, **131**
Food 25, 67
—allergy 123
—intolerance 124
—preference 69
—rewards 25, 102, 104,
   109, 153
—stealing 151
Foot care 78
France 12, 14, 30
Gender 41
—differences 21, 45
Germany 17
Ginger 20
Göncz, Mrs. 17
Grooming 17, 73
Havana Silk Dog 10
Havanese **13**
Health
—dental 122
—screenings 41
Heartworm 139-140, **141**
—life cycle **140**
—preventative 139
Heat cycle 21, 42
Heel 108
Hepatitis 119, 121
Hereditary eye disorders
   124

Hereditary skin disorders 122

Hiking 113

Holistic medicine 142-144

Home preparation for pup 48

Hookworm **137**

Hormone suppression 24

House-training 91-99

—schedule 98

Housing 92

Hunting instincts 17

Identification 82, 84

IGR 130, 132

Insect Growth Regulator 130, 132

Intelligence 17

Internal parasites 135-141

International Beauty Champion 27

International Champion 27

International Trial Champion 27

Judge 26, 111

Jumping 25, 58, 154

La Réunion 10, 14

Lead 53, 101

Legends 13

Leptospirosis 121

Lice **134**

Litter

—raising the 43

—size 42

—visiting a 41

Lupus 123

Madagascan Cotton Dog 10

Madagascar 10, 12-13, 30

—breeders of 14

—description of 11

—popularity on 20

Maltese 10, 13, **14**

Mange mite 134

Marking territory 22, 150

Mating 42

Maturity 69

Milk 68

Mite 79, 133

Motion sickness 82

Mounting 150-151

Mulch 61

Nail care 77-78

Name of breed 9, 14

Negative reinforcement 101

Neutering 22, 120, 150

Nipping 65

North America 14

Nutrition 72

Obedience class 86, 89, 111

Obedience competition 111

Obedience school 111

Obesity 24-25, 70, 72, 153

Off 154

OK 109

Old-dog syndrome 127

Origin of the breed 9, 13

Osteoarthritis 123

Otodectes cynotis 135

Pack behavior 17

Papillons 12

Parainfluenza 119

Parasite 128-141

—bites 122

—external 128-135

—internal 135-141

Parvovirus 119, 121

Patellar luxation 41

Pedigree 39

Persistent pupillary membrane 126

Personality 17-18, 25

Physical characteristics 18

Pollen allergy 123

Positive reinforcement 91, 101, 149

PPM 126

Praise 91, 102-104, 107, 110, 149

Preventative medicine 117

Psoroptes bovis **134**

Punishment 95, 101

Puppy

—appearance 40

—changes in personality 45

—development of 43

—diet 68

—first night home 60

—first trip to the vet 58

—health 41, 117

—introduction to family 59

—ownership 45

—preparing home for 48

—problems 62, 64

—selection 39-40, 42

—training 88

Puppy-proofing 57

Quiet 153

Rabies 121

Rare breed 12, 14, 40

Rawhide 53

RD 126

Recognition of breed —FCI 12

Registration 39

Retinal dysplasia 126

Rewards 25, 102, 104, 109, 153

Rhabditis **136**

Rhipicephalus sanguineus **135**

Roundworm **136**

Royal dog 12, 20

Russell, Dr. Robert Jay 14

Safety 49, 57, 66, 93, 95

—harness 81

Seasonal cycles 150

Senior diet 70, 121

Separation anxiety 66, 146-147

Sexual behavior 150

Shampoo 76

Show-quality 32

Showing

—preparation for 110

Sit 103

Sit/stay 105

Size 18

SKC 14, 40

Skin colors 12

Skin problems 121

Socialization 62, 64

Spaniels 13

Spaying 21-22, 120, 150

Specialty shows 30

Standard 26

—FCI 30

States Kennel Club 14, 40

Stay 105

Stealing food 151

Tapeworm **138**

Tear ducts 126

Teeth 44, 117, 120

Temperament 17-18, 25, 34, 117

Tenerife dog 10

Terriers 10 154

Thebromine 61

Thorndike's Theory of Learning 101

Thorndike, Dr. Edward 100

Threadworm 139

Tick 132-133

Tooth care 79

Toxocara canis 136

Toys 50, 52-54, 65-66, 93, 151

Tracheobronchitis 119

Training 25, 45

—commands 103

—consistency 64, 105

—crate 94

—equipment 101

—for agility 111

—for obedience 111

—for the show ring 110

Traveling 81-82

Treats 46, 102, 104, 109, 153

Trichuris vulpis 138

Tuléar 9, 14

UKC 40

United Kennel Club 40

—address 26

United States 14

United States of America Coton de Tuléar Club 14

Unser Kleinhund 18

Vacations 84

Vaccinations 59-60, 62-63, 117

Variable-ratio reward system 110

Veterinarian 58, 115, 121, 135

—specialist 122

Wandering 150

Water 71

Weaning 68, 117

Weight 18

Whining 61, 65

Whipworm 138-139

White 20

With children 24

World Dog Show 27, 30

My Coton de Tuléar

PUT YOUR PUPPY'S FIRST PICTURE HERE

Dog's Name _____

Date _____ Photographer _____